OLD TESTAMENT SURVEY

KEN HEMPHILL

Auxano
PRESS

Tigerville, South Carolina
www.AuxanoPress.com

Copyright 2012 by Ken Hemphill
All rights reserved.
Printed in the United States of America

Published by Auxano Press
Tigerville, South Carolina
www.AuxanoPress.com

All scripture quotations, unless otherwise indicated, are taken from the New American Standard Bible, Copyright 1960, 1962, 1963, 1968, 1971, 1972, 1973, 1975, 1977, 1995 by The Lockman Foundation. Used by permission. www.Lockman.org

Dedicated to
Lois Kenzie Boesch
A Beautiful Young Lady with
A Gentle Spirit and a
Great Faith

CONTENTS

Acknowledgments

A few years ago I wrote a little book entitled Core Convictions. As the title implies, it was a brief overview of the basic doctrines of the Christian faith. My good friend Don Wilton chose to study the book with all the youth and adults of his church family, First Baptist Spartanburg. He initially ordered two thousand copies, but the response was so overwhelming the church placed an additional order for five hundred. As the study progressed, Don asked me, "What's next?" He indicated that his people had expressed an interest in small-group materials that would cover basic biblical and doctrinal issues in a format that would allow them to build a basic Christian library.

That question led Auxano Press to undertake a project to provide sound biblical study material for small groups that would be "nondisposable," thus forming a foundation for a basic Christian library. The response from pastors and educators was enthusiastic, and thus this Survey of the Old Testament became an obvious starting point. A companion Survey of the New Testament by Dr. Kie Bowman will be available soon. You can anticipate an Old Testament and a New Testament book study each year, accompanied by a doctrinal study and a topical (practical) study.

Each lesson is written to stand alone, and yet the twelve lessons together will provide a biblical and exegetical study of the stated book, doctrine, or topic.

Each book is written for personal and/or small-group study. Study and administrative helps are available on-line at Auxanopress.com. The Auxano Press team prays that these materials will be used by the Holy Spirit to promote healthy personal and church growth.

Paula, my wife and partner in ministry, is my inspiration and sounding board. My children and grandchildren are the context for all my ministry of writing. Tina and Brett are the parents of Lois and Micah. Rachael and Trey are the parents of Emerson, Ward, and Ruby. Katie and Daniel are the parents of Aubrey, Sloane, and Edie. I pray that my writing will encourage them as they come to know Christ and grow to serve Him.

For the sake of simplicity and brevity, footnotes are kept to a minimum in this entire series of books. I have profited greatly from many fine commentaries, particularly The New American Commentary Series and the Tyndale Series. I am also indebted to Norman Geisler's A Popular Survey of the Old Testament.

Introduction

I begin this study with you with a word of grateful confession. I have always loved God's Word and have sought to hide it in my heart and allow it to be a guide to my path since I accepted Christ as my personal Savior at the age of nine. My dad was a preacher, and I grew up nurtured by people who believed God's Word without question. I will always be grateful for this rich scriptural heritage.

I was called to full-time vocational ministry while I was still a college student. Seminary was a natural next step for a young man who wanted to devote his life to teaching God's Word. My study at Southern Seminary was followed by graduate study at Cambridge under the gifted tutor Professor C. F. D. Moule. My ministry goal was to pastor, and after one year of teaching at Wingate College, I was privileged to begin my full-time pastoral ministry.

As I think back over the years of tutelage in my home and local church followed by seminary training and early ministry, I have come to realize that much of my focus in preaching and teaching has been in the New Testament, particularly in the Pauline letters. Like many other Christians, I was familiar with many of the Old Testament "stories" but spent little time studying or preaching from it. As a young pastor, I was convicted of this imbalance in my own preaching ministry. I soon began to plan regular preaching series that included significant passages from the Old Testament. I found that my study of the Old Testament not only developed a love for the first half of the Bible, but it enriched my understanding and love of the New Testament. Since the Bible has many authors but one Source, it should not surprise the reader that the message of the two Testaments forms a unified whole and must be studied together.

My ministry as an author led me to connect various Old Testament texts with their fulfillment in the New Testament. As I wrote The Names of God, I was enthralled to see that the various names for God were all completed in Christ. Preparing to write the seminal book for the Empowering Kingdom Growth initiative for the Southern Baptist Convention, I reread the Old Testament with a focus on the concept of God's kingdom. Once again I was moved to see that the kingdom teaching, which we often associate with Jesus and reflect on as we read the Gospels, was a consistent theme of the Old Testament. In truth it is impossible to appreciate fully Jesus' teaching on the King and His kingdom without a thorough understanding of its Old Testament background.

My passion for God's Word and His world have both been deepened as I have seen unfold the stories of creation, fall, and redemption from Genesis to Revelation. I have been challenged in my going and giving as I have been exposed to God's heart for the redemption of all nations from the beginning of time. I am humbled as I encounter man's rebellion (my own rebellion) and God's stubborn love and willingness to redeem and restore.

This study is in no way a comprehensive survey of the Old Testament. I have attempted to select texts that will provide the reader with a broad scope of the story line of the Old Testament. Many of the selected texts correspond with texts that mission personnel often used to "story the gospel" from creation to Christ. Another person attempting to write a similar book could well have chosen other texts and made a case for their inclusion.

Each lesson is written so that it stands alone, but prayerfully the twelve studies when taken together should give the reader a clear overview of the story line of the Old Testament. Each lesson ends with a Scripture verse for memory and meditation. I recommend that you use these as you study this book, either alone or in a small-group context. Memorizing these twelve verses should enable you to keep in memory the big picture of God's redemptive history. Free Scripture memory cards are available online from Auxanopress.com.

It is my prayer that God will use this study to provide information that leads to transformation. I am praying that you will find your place in God's redemptive history. I am praying that this little survey will help you understand the story line of the Old Testament and have a deep desire to study each book in greater depth.

Read this book with your Bible by your side and with the prayer that the Holy Spirit will be your teacher.

The Creation
FOCAL TEXT: GENESIS 1-2

CHAPTER 1

"In the beginning God created the heavens and the earth" (Gen. 1:1).

"The Cosmos *is all that is or ever will be. . . . Our obligation to survive is owed not just to ourselves but also to that Cosmos, ancient and vast, from which we spring."—Carl Sagan (Cosmos, 4, 345).*

These two statements create quite a contrast. One begins with God; the other, with the cosmos. They point to two radically different worldviews with far-reaching consequences. The Bible begins with an account of the creation of the world and man who inhabits it. The implications are profound and life changing. If the world, and all life in it, is a gift of a benevolent Creator, then it must be managed according to the dictates of the Creator. If man is created in God's image, then life itself has great value and must be used wisely and preserved at all costs. One can see how this impacts our understanding of the value of the life of the handicapped, the terminally ill, and the unborn. Yes, much is at stake in the discussion of the origin of life. God begins His revelation of Himself to humankind with the story of "the beginnings."

In the Beginning
Genesis 1:1

"In the beginning" is not simply an introductory phrase like "once upon a time." It is a solemn affirmation that God created everything from nothing (*ex nihilo*). On eighteen occasions when the Hebrew word behind this translation is used, it is translated the same way— "in the beginning." However, it can be translated as "choice" or "firstfruits."[1] In other words, God's creation is God's gift to Himself. Creation was the "firstfruits" of His divine activity.

This understanding of these familiar words only scratches the surface of the deep truths imbedded within them. (1) "In the beginning" means there is more to come and that everything was created with intentionality and purpose by the One who existed before anything was. (2) "In the beginning" declares that the creation of the heavens and the earth was initiated with an ultimate goal in mind. They have meaning and purpose. God the Creator controls both the beginning and the end, moving everything toward His ultimate kingdom purpose. The prophet Isaiah spoke of this truth: "Remember the former things long past, for I am God, and there is no one like Me, declaring the end from the beginning ... and I will accomplish all My good pleasure" (Isa. 46:9–11). (3) "In the beginning" means that the Creator is the Owner of all that exists. Whenever the word create is used in the Old Testament, it speaks of divine activity.

---

1 Enhanced Strong's Lexicon, *7, 225.*

This truth has a profound impact on how we view nature and all material things.

God
Genesis 1:1

God is the subject of the first sentence of the Bible. This word jumps from the page as it dominates the entire first chapter, being used thirty-two times in thirty-one verses, not counting the pronouns that refer back to God. This first chapter, the remainder of Genesis, and the entire Bible are about the God who created everything and revealed Himself to man. To read this chapter or this book without seeing God as the focal point is to misread this book.

Creation is not only an act of God; rightly understood it bears witness to Him and His character. Paul states it thus, "For since the creation of the world His invisible attributes, His eternal power and divine nature, have been clearly seen, being understood through what has been made, so that they are without excuse" (Rom. 1:20). When we observe the complex and uniquely balanced world, we conclude that an Intelligent Designer was at work. When we observe human life, we conclude that the designer is personal, moral, and knowable. The whole of creation and the Bible speak of the wonder of a sovereign God who desires to be known, loved, and praised by those whom He created. The brief account of creation in Genesis is less concerned with the questions of how and when than with who and why. While it contains reliable scientific affirmations, its focus is on theology rather than biology or geology.

Created
Genesis 1:1

The subject of creation is always God; everything else is a direct object of God's creative activity. Whenever the word create is used in the Old Testament, it speaks of divine activity. It means "to originate, to bring into being something distinctively new out of nothing, to bring to perfection." Only sovereign God has the power to create and to bring to perfect completion. Throughout the Bible creation is the unique activity reserved for God alone.

The creation narrative is written in two parts that are complementary and not contradictory. The first section (1:1–2:3) is focused on God the Creator; the second part (2:4–24) is focused toward the earth and man. The first underlines the sovereign power of God; the second declares that the chief goal of creation is to lead to communion between the Creator and man, the crown of God's creation.

In case you are wondering, the concept of divine creation is not confined to the book of Genesis. References to creation are found throughout the whole of Scripture. The word created is found twenty times in Isaiah 40–66. When you read those chapters, you will discover the prophet was intent on distinguishing between Israel's God as the true Lord of history in contrast to the Babylonian practices of idolatry and astrology.

The language of creation is also found in the New Testament as we have seen by our quote from Paul in Romans 1:20. John, in his Gospel, gives us a glimpse of the time before creation, "In the beginning was the Word, and the Word was with God, and the Word was God. . . . All things came into being through Him, and apart from Him nothing came into begin that has come into being" (John 1:1, 3). The writer to the Hebrews declares: "By faith we understand that the worlds were prepared by the word of God, so that what is seen was not made out of things which are visible" (11:3).

The truth that "God created" not only appears throughout Scripture, but it also has profound implications on all of life. It affirms that the Creator has the right and responsibility to ensure that His creation serves His purposes. A proper understanding of creation should motivate us to respond in worship. Look at Psalm 95:3, 6: "For the Lord is a great God and a great King above all gods, in whose hand are the depths of the earth, the peaks of the mountains are His also. . . . Come, let us worship and bow down, let us kneel before the Lord our Maker." Further, it assures us that we can and must depend on Him for everything. When the Lord answered the long-suffering Job in the midst of his trials, he pointed him back to creation. "Where were you when I laid the foundation of the earth? Tell Me, if you have understanding" (Job 38:4). The bottom line of God's message to Job is that He created the earth and therefore is capable of managing it and all the affairs of Job's life. Is it encouraging to know the Creator cares about you?

The Earth and Everything in It
Genesis 1:3–5

Creation begins with light, which is deemed to be "good" (1:3–5). God then separates water and dry land creating the seas, once again declaring it to be "good" (1:6–10). This is followed in turn by vegetation, the sun and moon, the animals of the sea, the animals of the land, and finally man. You may have noticed the phrase "God said" repeated throughout this section. God calls everything into being by eight specific commands. This makes clear that the universe is not self-existent; it did not struggle to create itself, nor is it simply a divine emanation. God's thought created the minutest detail of all that exists, and His Word called it into being.

At the end of each day of creation, God declares what He has made to be "good." Following the final act of creation, where God creates man in His own image, we read of God's reaction: "God saw all that He made, and behold, it was very good" (1:31a). "Good" is not to be understood in terms of God's patting Himself on the back in awestruck wonder at the beauty of His own creation. "Good" means that everything God made reflects His character since it comes from Him and serves His purpose. Everything is given value and meaning by its relationship to its Creator. God is also the sole judge of His own creative activity and the subsequent use of the resources He has provided. This leads us to our final topic: that man is distinguished from all other created things by the affirmation that God created him, male and female, in His own image (1:26–27).

Man in the Image of God
Genesis 1:26–27; 2:7, 18–24

Whenever you are feeling insignificant, undervalued, or unimportant, read this section of Genesis and absorb this truth: *God created you in His image and gave you stewardship over all His creation*. The creation of humankind is the climax of the creation week in Genesis 1. Humans are like God in a manner that no other earthly creatures are. We have the capability and opportunity to relate to Him and replicate, at an earthly level, the holy ways of God. Every human life is sacred, and each of us was created with purpose.

In Genesis 2:7 we read: "The Lord God formed man of dust from the ground, and breathed into his nostrils the breath of life; and man became a living being." Man, created from the earth has a material body that is given life by a nonmaterial, personal self, which the Bible speaks of as a "soul" or "spirit." Man is an integrated whole and his/her redemption impacts body, soul, and spirit.

God's image is equally shared by man and woman. The complementary nature of the two genders is designed to lead to enriching cooperation as they together manage and replenish the earth (2:18–23).

Man in God's image is relational, rational, and therefore responsible. Persons are created to live in harmonious relationship with one another. God declares, "It is not good for man to be alone" (2:18). We demand and desire the fellowship of others like ourselves. The most intimate earthly union possible is one man and one woman as husband and wife (2:24).

But man's greatest relational need is to live in unhindered intimacy with his/her Creator. In the innocence of the garden, the man and woman experienced immediate communion with God. Simply stated, we cannot live fully without God because we were created by Him and for Him.

Rational man has the ability to understand and respond to God as He reveals Himself to us. Man's rational capacity makes him/her fully responsible. God's first words to the man and woman were words of blessing followed by an assignment (1:28). Man is God's steward and thus becomes accountable for managing God's resources according to His standards and for His purposes.

As God's stewards over all other created things, we are God's representatives on earth. In the New Testament Paul speaks of redeemed man as an ambassador for Christ (2 Cor. 5:20). Man's highest purpose is to advance God's kingdom by His power and for His glory to the ends of the earth until His return. Man's ultimate destiny is to serve God as a royal priesthood forever (Rev. 1:6).

For Memory and Meditation

"In the beginning God created the heavens and the earth." Genesis 1:1

The Fall of Man

CHAPTER 2

FOCAL TEXT: GENESIS 3:1-24

Can you imagine a place where every human need is provided for, and man is allowed direct and unrestricted access to his/her Creator? Does it seem too good to be true? Even today we speak of beautiful, idyllic situations as being like the garden of Eden.

We must not, however, allow such references to Eden cause us to think of the story of the garden as little more than a symbolic or mythological way to talk about the beginning of time. Both the Old and New Testaments assume its reality and argue from it, making the first Adam as literal as the last. Luke traces Jesus' genealogy to Adam (3:23). Paul consistently speaks of Adam as "one man" and his sin as "one trespass" (Rom. 5:18–19; 1 Cor. 15:20–21). The New Testament, however, makes clear that the story of the fall is not simply the narrative of one man's fall; it is the story of how sin and death entered into the world (Rom. 5:12).

The world we live in is far different from the garden of Eden. Something drastic has happened to the created order, which God declared to be "very good." Instead of a joyful gathering of natural resources, we find ourselves struggling to scratch out a living. Rather than enjoying immediate and full intimacy with God, we wonder about His existence and care. What happened to Eden?

The Enticing Offer
Genesis 3:1–5, 15

Without any formal introduction "the serpent" arrives on the scene. Verse 1 leaves no question that the serpent was part of God's creation. Evil has no existence of its own and thus does not, of its own initiative, invade God's creation. Evil is the result of the rebellion of God's creatures, and the consequences of such rebellion is always catastrophic. The craftiness of the serpent suggests he was a tool of the great adversary of man, the devil. This identification of the serpent and the great adversary becomes more explicit in Genesis 3:15 but is only fully revealed in the New Testament (Rev. 20:2).

The tempter begins his attack with a question that contains a suggestion rather than an outright accusation. "Indeed, has God said, 'You shall not eat from any tree of the garden'?" (3:1). The implication is clear—a loving God wouldn't withhold anything good from man. The question is an obvious distortion of the single prohibition God made concerning the trees of the garden. In Genesis 2:16 we discover that man is given the freedom to eat freely from any tree of the garden with the singular exception of the tree of the knowledge of good and evil (2:17). This tree stands as a symbol of God's authority, reminding Adam and Eve that their freedom is not absolute but must be exercised within God's guidelines. The serpent's question appeals to man's pride, implying that God's Word and God's way are subject to human judgment.

Eve is drawn into the adversary's web. She agrees with

the tempter, even adding to and exaggerating God's restriction, telling the serpent that God has said, "You shall not eat from it or touch it" (vv. 2–3). Eve is joined by many people today who focus on God's prohibitions rather than His gracious gifts.

All subtlety is now jettisoned as the adversary contradicts the word of God: "You surely will not die!" (3:4). The woman must now choose to believe the word of the serpent or the word of God. Notice that the first two doctrines to be brought into question are the truth of God's word and the reality of man's accountability and judgment. We hear it in the assertion, "Surely a loving God would not allow man to . . ." Why would Eve take the word of a liar rather than trusting the works and words of loving God who created her and provided for her every need? Why do we? When we reject God's Word and rely on our own understanding, we are actually siding with the adversary.

The tempter suggests that God is jealous of man and desires to keep him subservient. "For God knows that in the day you eat from it your eyes will be opened, and you will be like God, knowing good and evil" (3:5). It is intoxicating to think that we can be "little gods" and in the process outwit the one true God. The moment man buys into this lie, God becomes a rival who keeps man in his place with unnecessary and unloving restrictions. Quite a contrast to the God of the Bible who takes upon Himself human flesh and becomes a servant, even to the point of death on a cross (Phil. 2:7).

The Devastating Fall
Genesis 3:6

Verse 6 records the fall of man in such simple terms that we are astounded to read that man would so quickly rebel against his/her Creator. Do you hear in this verse the subtle progression of sin? Eve saw that the fruit was delightful to look at, she desired it, and thus she took it. We all struggle with this same progression of sin. Sin begins with sight, which creates desire. Desire leads us to conclude that we need it, deserve it, or just want it, and so we take it. John, in his first epistle, speaks of the progression of desire combined with pride. "For all that is in the world, the lust of the flesh and the lust of the eyes and the boastful pride of life, is not from the Father, but is from the world" (1 John 2:16).

Derek Kidner has summarized the fall succinctly: "The pattern of sin runs right through the act. For Eve listened to a creature instead of the Creator, followed her impressions against her instructions, and made self-fulfillment her goal. This prospect of material, aesthetic, and mental enrichment (6a) seemed to add up to life itself."[1]

Adam, rather than taking the lead in obedience and righteousness, followed his wife into sin. They bought the lie! They believed they could rely on their own wisdom rather than obeying God's Word. They believed they could be their own master.

---

1 Derek Kidner, Tyndale Old Testament Commentary, *Genesis, vol. 1* (Downers Grove, IL: InterVarsity Press, 1967), 53.

The Staggering Consequences
Genesis 3:5, 8–19

The results of their sin are immediate and far-reaching. The serpent's promise that their eyes would be opened (v. 5) was fulfilled, but it was far from the beatific enlightenment they anticipated. They now saw a familiar and beautiful world from the lens marred by sin, and thus they projected evil onto innocence causing them to feel shame. This new-felt sense of shame caused them to cover their nakedness and to attempt to hide themselves from the presence of God (v. 8). Before the fall they enjoyed intimate personal relationship with God, but now shame led to separation from the One who created them and provided for all their needs.

Adam and Eve first hear the sound of the Lord walking in the garden before they hear His voice (v. 8). Needlessly, they attempt to hide themselves from an omniscient and omnipresent God. Notice that God takes the initiative, calling out to man, "Where are you?" (v. 9). God is not lacking knowledge, and therefore we must hear in these words as a gracious invitation from a loving God. God's desire is to draw man to Himself rather than drive him further into hiding. Adam responds, "I was afraid because I was naked" (v. 10b). After shame, fallen man's next emotion is fear. Shame and an irrational fear of a benevolent Creator are still elements of man's fallen condition.

In verses 12–13 we discover that sin also impacts the couple's relationship with each other as they each began to blame the other for the act of rebellion. Both Adam and Eve place the ultimate blame for their sin on God. Adam accuses God for his transgression since God gave him the woman. Eve, in turn, points to the serpent that God created.

Pain and suffering now enter the world and the life of our first couple and every couple who follow after them. The woman's punishment is directly related to her unique childbearing role which enabled her to fulfill God's command to replenish the earth (Gen. 1:28; 3:16). Man's punishment is likewise related to his role as caretaker of the creation. Now man's toil will be frustrated by the presence of thorns and thistles (3:17–19). Further, the phrases "your desire will be for your husband" and "he will rule over you" (v. 16) point to a marriage relationship that has degenerated from a fully intimate and personal partnership to that of passion, competition, and domination. Man's ultimate end will be death: "For you are dust, and to dust you shall return" (v. 19).

The Amazing Love of God
Genesis 3:9, 15, 22–24

We have already noticed the gracious act of God who sought man, calling out to him, while he was still attempting to hide himself from God (v. 9). There are other indications that God is determined not to abandon man in his sinful condition. Verse 15 has often been referred to as a first glimpse at the gospel, the first promise of a coming Redeemer (Messiah), His suffering and ultimate triumph over the evil one. The gospel bursts on the scene as God passes sentence on the enemy of man.

"And I will put enmity between you and the woman, and between your seed and her seed; he shall bruise you on the head, and you shall bruise him on the heel." Redemption is not merely an issue of man's need as it is an issue of God's rule (cf. Col. 2:14–15).

The conflict between the seed of Satan and the seed of the woman points to the coming conflict between Jesus the Messiah and the demonic forces of the adversary. Further, wicked persons are sometimes spoken of in terms of being sons (seed) of the adversary (cf. Matt. 13:38–39 and John 8:44). We can rightly see here the events of the cross where Satan bruised the heel of the seed of woman (Jesus) but in the same moment was himself crushed by the force of the heel. The cross, which appeared to be crushing defeat, was, in fact, stunning victory. Satan's hostility was defeated by Christ's humility.

Here, in the apparent gloom of judgment, are the rays of mercy and hope. Adam named his wife "Eve" meaning "life" (v, 20), suggesting that Adam heard the promise of verse 15 with the ears of faith. There may be a touch of irony in the statement that "man has become like one of Us" (v. 22). Adam and Eve had desired a status of sovereignty—knowing good and evil—a status they could never achieve. Their attempted intrusion into this realm was a denial of their creaturely status and rebellion against the uniqueness of God. Therefore man must be cut off from the tree of life so that he will not become forever fixed in his rebellion. What appears to be merely punishment is an act of grace.

Man was driven from the garden of Eden by decree and necessity. Eternal life is fellowship with God, which man in his rebellion has repudiated. The garden was then secured by cherubim and a flaming sword that turns in every direction (v. 24). Adam and Eve's way back into the garden was made impassable, indicating that man cannot, by any means, save himself. The cherubim will be seen again as symbolic guardians of the holy of holies. Their image was embroidered on the veil that barred access to the holy of holies, and they were modeled above the ark (Exod. 36:35; 37:7–9).

Matthew tells us that, at the death of Christ, the veil separating man from the holy of holies was torn in two from top to bottom (Matt. 27:51). The writer of Hebrews explains the significance: "Therefore, brethren, since we have confidence to enter the holy place by the blood of Jesus, by a new and living way which He inaugurated for us through the veil, that is, His flesh, and since we have a great priest over the house of God" (10:19–21).

The "wages of sin is death," but God's gift "is eternal life" through His Son (Rom. 6:23). What man can never achieve by his own effort has been made available in Christ Jesus. Have you entered into the holy place by accepting Christ's death on your behalf?

For Memory and Meditation

"And I will put enmity between you and the woman, and between your seed and her seed; he shall bruise you on the head, and you shall bruise him on the heel." Genesis 3:15

The Flood

Fascination concerning the flood and Noah's ark remains unabated. Despite political challenges and grueling conditions, expeditions are still mounted to climb the icy slopes of Mount Ararat on the borders of modern-day Turkey and Armenia in an attempt to find the remains of Noah's great boat. Some doubt such expeditions will ever yield results since the mountain we call Mount Ararat may not be the same location as the one mentioned in the Bible. The identity of the "sons of God" (6:2) and the Nephilim (6:4) continues to be a matter of active interest and debate. Whatever conclusion we might reach concerning such matters from a distance of thousands of years, we should not allow the debate over obscure facts to cause us to miss the profound story of the character of God, His righteous judgment of sin, and His stunning provision of grace contained in this story.

Man's Rebellion and Fall
Genesis 6:1–8

The first section of the flood narrative is summarized by verse 5: "Then the Lord saw that the wickedness of man was great on the earth, and that every intent of the thoughts of his heart was only evil continually." This assessment is echoed again in verses 11–12 with the word "corrupt" being repeated three times in these two short verses.

However one understands verse 2, which speaks of the sons of God taking wives of the daughters of men, the point is clear—evil and depravity have reached an entirely new level as man has jettisoned all mores of sexual purity. Men did not select their wives on the basis of faith but on simple sexual impulse without regard to the spiritual values of the women in question. Each person was acting on sheer animal passion because "every intent of the thoughts of his heart was only evil continually." Paul, in Romans 7:18, agrees with this assessment of fallen man, indicating that "nothing good" can be found in the fallen nature of man. The integral connection of one's thoughts and behavior—the thoughts of one's heart—will ultimately be expressed in one's behavior.

God's response to man's sin is one of great sorrow. Verse 6 indicates that God was "grieved in His heart." God suffers because of man's sin, but a holy God cannot tolerate sin because it kills and destroys those who are created in His own image. A holy God can do nothing other than to bring judgment on sin. Sin's destructive power is so great that it must be dealt with completely. Thus the Lord has determined: "I will blot out man whom I have created from the face of the land" (6:7a). God does not glory or take delight in the impending act of judgment. Listen to the agony in the words "for I am sorry that I made them" (6:7).

The simplicity and brevity of verse 8—"But Noah found favor in the eyes of the Lord"—must be heard against the agony of verse 7. Against the backdrop of impending judgment comes the promise of redemption and grace. While God is grieved with sin, He is not angry with man. At the very moment He must pronounce judgment upon sin, He is thinking in terms of grace and redemption. We err when we think God is disinterested in the affairs of men or that He is harsh in judging His creation. His judgment springs from His righteous character and His indignation with sin. Nonetheless, it contains the promise of grace. Peter, who uses the story of the flood to discuss the affairs of man, tells us that it is not God's desire that any should perish but that all should come to repentance (2 Pet. 3:9).

God's Provision
Genesis 6:5, 9–7:24; 8:1–22; 9:1–17

Does the phrase, "These are the records of the generations of Noah" (6:9), remind you of 5:1—"This is the book of the generations of Adam"? It should, for this verse opens a new section of the book of Genesis, which is anticipated by the startling announcement of a righteous remnant in verse 8. In a sense these words announce a new beginning, a new world that will be populated by eight precious souls (1 Pet. 3:20)--the household of Noah, a man who was righteous. In a world totally out of step with God, one man walked with God (6:9). "Righteous" speaks of Noah's reputation with man while "blameless" speaks of his standing before God.

The following account is often referred to as the story of the flood, but it is more accurately seen as the story of God's personal and gracious dealing with mankind.

Noah is the prominent character in the story because of his radical obedience to God's commands. The story is relatively straightforward as God gives Noah a series of commands that will enable him to survive the coming judgment (6:13–7:5) and the execution of that judgment through the flood (7:6–24). Through obedience he will be allowed to experience God's mercy seen in the dissipation of the flood (8:1–22) and enter into a covenant of promise (9:1–17).

Verses 10–12 of chapter 6 again summarize what was said in the closing chapter of the record of the old world, the generations of Adam (6:5). The repetition of the word "corrupted," which can also be translated "destroyed," suggests that what God has determined to destroy with the flood has been essentially self-destroyed by the choices of sinful man.

An earth "filled with violence" (6:13) could not continue unabated, and therefore God tells Noah that He is going to destroy man and the earth. The earth was destroyed in the sense that it was unable to support life during the time the floodwaters covered the earth. Noah and his family had to make provision for repopulating the earth by taking a pair of each animal about the ark. The ark or "chest" was designed with a singular purpose, to provide continued existence for a variety of creatures. Its shape required no launching.

The effort of building the ark and collecting two of every species of animal would have been an incredibly laborious task. One can only imagine the ridicule Noah encountered from his wicked neighbors as he constructed a massive boat and warned them of impending judgment by means of a flood.

God, who can create everything out of nothing, could have devised a means of judging sin and saving the righteous without the aid of Noah and his family. The partnership between God and man demonstrates God's plan to allow man to participate as a co-laborer with Him in His redemptive work. Further, Peter indicates that the lengthy time required to build the ark was a manifestation of God's patience, who "kept waiting in the days of Noah, during the construction of the ark" (1 Pet. 3:20). As he worked, Noah preached righteousness (2 Pet. 2:5). Noah's neighbors were given adequate warning but rejected God's appeals through Noah. God always warns before He judges because He desires that none should perish (2 Pet. 3:9). We should never mistake God's patience for His lack of attention or concern.

God's Covenant Promise
Genesis 6:16, 18; 7:1–5, 16;
8:16–17; 9:1, 10, 12–17

The term *covenant* is an important biblical term to speak of God's relationship with His people. The first occurrence of this word is found in Genesis 6:18: "But I will establish My covenant with you; and you shall enter the ark—you and your sons and your, and your sons' wives with you." Noah and his immediate family are not merely survivors of the flood; they are the vessels of God's promise for a new world.

The story of the flood is replete with images of God's

faithfulness in providing for man's redemption.

- The construction of the ark called for a window near the roof (6:16) providing for inner illumination and serving as a symbol where Noah and his family would "see" an end to the time of judgment.

- The door, which extended to all three decks, was the means by which God sealed Noah's family in the ark (7:16) and would be the access for Noah and his family to enter the new world when the flood subsided. God extends a personal invitation for Noah and his family to enter the ark. "Enter the ark, you and all your household, for you alone I have seen to be righteous before Me in this time" (7:1). In the New Testament, Jesus used "door" as an image of the Good Shepherd's provision for His sheep. They must enter into salvation and safety through Him alone (John 10:1–9).

- The careful provision of the ark to meet all of Noah's needs (7:1–5) speaks of God's abundant and personal provision for all of man's needs.

As the floodwater subsides and the earth is once again suitable for habitation, God invites Noah to exit the ark and inhabit the new world. "Go out of the ark, you and your wife and your sons and your son's wives with you. Bring out with you every living thing of all flesh that is with you, birds and animals and every creeping thing that creeps on the earth, that they may breed abundantly on the earth, and be fruitful and multiply on the earth" (8:16–17). God specifically instructs Noah and his sons, "Be fruitful and multiply, and fill the earth" (9:1). With a promise and a command, Noah, like a new Adam, is placed in a virgin world washed clean from sin.

In some ways the spectacular deliverance by the ark is seen as a preliminary event leading to new life as Noah and his family enter a new creation. Peter compares the flood with baptism as the provision of a way through death into life (1 Pet. 3:21). Peter reminds his readers that redemption is not the result of the physical baptism—"not the removal of dirt from the flesh"— but is accomplished through a clean heart the result of the resurrection of Christ. In the same manner the ark brought Noah and his family through the flood to a new life, Christ alone can bring us from death to new life.

Appropriately, Noah's first thoughts upon exiting the ark are of the God of redemption, and therefore his first act is to build an altar and offer a sacrifice to the Lord. Noah's resources to provide for himself and his family were limited, and his task of repopulating the earth was immense. It would have been easy to rationalize that a costly sacrifice at this time would not be wise. But Noah's gratitude was such that worship was spontaneous. The sacrifice was a pleasing aroma to the Lord who promises never to destroy the earth in the same manner.

Chapter 9 provides more specifics of God's covenant with Noah. To give a regular reminder of His covenant, He set a bow in the sky (9:12–17). Each time people see the bow, they are to remember God's covenant. The bow arises from the conjunction of sun and storm as judgment and mercy are joined together in the story of the flood. God's first explicit covenant is stunning in its breadth, its permanence, and its generosity. It encompasses every living creature (9:10). It is perpetual since it is promised to Noah and all his descendants. It is gracious because it was unconditional and undeserved.

Lessons from the Flood
Genesis 9:16

The flood was prompted by man's rebellion against God. That rebellion was manifest in man's thoughts and actions. Man sometimes mistakes God's long-suffering patience for a lack of concern. Holy God will not tolerate sin but will surely bring judgment even though it grieves His heart. God patiently waits with desire that all should come to repentance, but many come under judgment because they reject God, shutting Him out of their lives. God provides a way for those who walk with Him to escape judgment, and He freely enters into a personal covenant relationship with them.

For Memory and Meditation

"When the bow is in the cloud, then I will look upon it, to remember the everlasting covenant between God and every living creature of all flesh that is on the earth." Genesis 9:16

24

The Call of Abraham, the Choice of a People
FOCAL TEXT: GENESIS 11-13

We have seen the continuing impact of the fall as man sought his own pleasure and ignored his Creator. Sexual sin and disobedience became so pervasive on earth that God provided a new beginning through the flood. Tragically, man continues to live in outright rebellion, and sin continues unabated.

Primeval history reaches its fruitless climax with the construction of the tower of Babel as man aspires to glorify himself by securing a way to heaven by his own efforts (Gen. 11:1–9). The project is grandiose: "Come, let us build for ourselves a city, and a tower whose top will reach into heaven, and let us make ourselves a name" (11:4a). The motivating force behind such a bold project is man's insecurity—"Otherwise we will be scattered abroad over the face of the whole earth" (11:4b). The tower of Babel stands as a monument to man's continuing attempt to control his own destiny. The city of Babylon is used throughout Scripture to symbolize godless society with all its pleasures, dissipations, and superstitions (cf. Isa. 47:8–13; Rev. 17–18). Mankind, designed to relate to and to depend on God, had united in their attempt to glorify themselves as deity. To bring judgment and demonstrate that human unity apart from God was superficial, God introduced confusion into human communication and scattered the people over the face of the earth (11:7–9). Ironically, even in man's rebellion, God is causing man to fulfill the creation mandate to "fill the earth." Even man's sin and rebellion can be made to serve God's purposes.

God is tenacious and tender when it comes to the redemption of man, and thus He selects a people to join Him in a reconciliation process that would establish true unity among all peoples. The genealogy of the descendants of Shem (11:10–31) leads us out of the old world into the era of the patriarchs which begins with Abram (Abraham) and culminates in Joseph. The genealogy of Shem moves us from Noah to Abram, the next major character of the redemption story.

The call of Abraham signals God's intention to work through a chosen people to bring blessing to all the nations of the earth so that all people groups, scattered by sin and rebellion (11:7–9), can be united once again as they are restored to their rightful King. The story of God's chosen people dominates the remainder of the book of Genesis and centers first on a son of promise (Isaac) and then on a land of promise (Canaan). After the birth of Isaac, we follow the line of succession as God's selection of the younger sons demonstrates both His grace and His sovereignty. The patriarchal period ends in Egypt as God provides for His people and reveals His plan for the unique role of Israel as priestly people who will advance God's kingdom on earth.

A Call and a Response
Genesis 11:27, 30; 12:1

Abram is first introduced in 11:27 as one of the three sons of Terah. We are told that he married Sarai who was barren and had no child (11:30). The repetition of "barren" and "had no child" underscores Sarai's helpless condition and God's gracious and miraculous provision for the child of promise.

The story of creation began with God speaking—"Let there be light" (1:3), and now the story of redemption begins in like manner—"Now the Lord said to Abram" (12:1). God commands Abram to leave his own country and relatives to travel to a land He will show him. The call to forsake all and follow finds its nearest parallel in the Gospels when Jesus challenges His "would be" followers to abandon all and follow Him. God's covenant with Abram and his descendants (Israel) was, from the beginning, a matter of faith and not law. Paul makes this same point in the book of Galatians. "Even so Abraham believed God, and it was reckoned to him as righteousness" (Gal. 3:6). He concludes that those who are of the faith are blessed with Abraham, "the believer" (3:9).

The call, first heard by Abram in Mesopotamia (Acts 7:2–4), requires that Abram leave the familiar and the comfortable in exchange for the unknown and the demanding. The destination of the land God has promised to provide has yet to be revealed, and thus Abram is required to exercise faith (cf. Heb. 11:8). The call of God ultimately leaves the recipient of that call with the necessity of choice and the resulting demand of obedience.

God has chosen to establish a divine-human partnership rather than a divine dictatorship in order to establish His rule on earth. He has chosen to work through an obedient people to expand His kingdom on earth.

Ur, the place Abram must abandon, was a well-developed city with two- and three-story houses built around pleasant courtyards. The people were well educated, and the design of the ziggurat reveals architectural sophistication of the much later Parthenon in Athens. The thousands of clay tables, which have been unearthed in this area, provide details of the well-developed cultural, business, and legal aspects of life in Ur. The primary deity of Ur was the moon god, Nanna, for whom the ziggurat was built. Joshua tells us that Abram's father "served other gods" (24:2).[1] To heed the call of God, Abram must leave his home, comfort, and family religion.

God still uses and calls individuals to join Him in His kingdom activity. He still demands trust and its resulting obedience. Those who choose to join Him will seldom know the ultimate destination of their earthly journey. Such knowledge is unnecessary! All we need to know is whom we are following.

Blessed to Bless
Genesis 12:2–3

The call to follow God is accompanied by a threefold promise. Read Genesis 12:2–3 aloud and listen to the

---

1 D. Stuart Briscoe, The Communicator's Commentary: Genesis (Waco, TX: Word, 1987), 122–23.

repetition of "I will." The "I will" promises assure Abram that his radical act of obedience will have eternal consequences and global impact: (1) The man who had been unable to father a child will become the father of a great nation. (2) He would receive God's blessing, which consists of His presence, His provision, and His protection. (3) This obscure man from Ur of the Chaldeans is promised that God will make his name "great." In this regard Abram stands in marked contrast to the arrogant people who came to ruin because they sought to "make for ourselves a name" (11:4) apart from God. Radical obedience then and now is rewarded with God's blessing, which enables us to join God in His kingdom activity.

But God's blessing is not to be hoarded and consumed by Abram and his descendants; it is to be shared. Abram has the unique privilege of blessing others. It is stated matter-of-factly in Genesis 12:2: "And so you shall be a blessing," inferring that the natural outcome of receiving from the hand of God is the privilege of giving to others. The scope of Abram's blessing is further articulated in verse 3: "And in you all the families of the earth will be blessed." The nations that have been scattered because of human pride will be gathered to their rightful King by those blessed to join God in His redemptive work. It is impossible to read verse 3 without thinking of the Great Commission in Matthew 28:19–20 where the command to disciple the nations is given to the disciples of the resurrected Lord.

This call and commission to bless the nations was only marginally understood and embraced by Israel. This theme virtually disappears between the patriarchs and the kings, apart from the reminder of this priestly role once again articulated by God through Moses at Mount Sinai (Exod. 19:5–6). The psalmist and some of the later prophets remind Israel of this high calling and responsibility of "blessing the nations," but it never became a major emphasis or plan of action until the ascension of the Messiah King. Israel often seemed content to consume the blessing of God rather than convey it to the nations, preferring the privilege to the responsibility.

Abram Begins a Journey of Faith
Genesis 12:4, 6–8, 16–18, 20

The simplicity of verse 4 should not cause us to overlook the profundity of the action. "So Abram went forth as the Lord had spoken to him; and Lot went with him. Now Abram was seventy-five years old when he departed from Haran." Without a clear destination in mind, Abram responds to the promise God had spoken to him. What journey of faith have you undertaken that was based solely on what God said to you about your role in His kingdom purpose?

Abram's faith is quickly tested as he meets the Canaanite who "was then in the land" (12:6). No doubt these people who inhabited Canaan would not have been overly hospitable to a man who believed that he had been given possession of the land they now occupied. We know from history that the Canaanites would be a perennial enemy, and their idolatrous religious practices would be a constant temptation for the Israelites.

Abram seems unperturbed as he is fortified once again by the Lord's presence and His promise: "'To your descendants I will give this land.' So he built an altar there to the Lord who had appeared to him" (12:7). This act of humble worship was not a singular response of the grateful Abram. In verse 8 we are told that after worshipping at Shechem he proceeded to the mountain on the east of Bethel, "and there he built an altar to the Lord and called upon the name of the Lord." The word translated "Lord" is the memorial name, "Yahweh," which will be more fully explained in Exodus 3. But it is already clear that Abram's action of building altars was a symbolic planting of a flag which declared that Yahweh was Lord over all the land and all the nations. The only structures Abram left behind as he followed the voice of God were altars, places of worship.

Abram's journey is not simple or easy as his faith and resolve are tested once again by a famine in the land. No doubt the close proximity of Egypt, which was watered by the flooding of the Nile, must have seemed like an obvious refuge for his family. Yet we should recall that God had promised to provide for his needs. The text nowhere suggests that Abram enquired of God concerning this decision to seek provision in Egypt. Abram appears to have made this decision of his own initiative, and the consequences are immediate. Frightened for their safety, Abram convinces Sarai to lie about her identity.

Are you surprised to see how quickly one can move from a journey of faith to a detour of fear? Abram is caught up in his own web of deception and is unable to refuse Pharaoh's rich provisions (12:16) or answer his question about why he chose to lie to him (12:18). The significance of the story has to do with God's ability to provide what He promised concerning a land and a people. At the first sign of hunger, Abram relies on his own cunning rather than turn to God. Through his deceit Abram, who was to be a blessing to the nations, brought plagues upon the Egyptians (12:17). It took deportation by a pagan pharaoh to get Abram back to Canaan (12:20).

I am glad God's Word records the story of Abram's faith journey including the embarrassing moments when fear and unbelief caused him to become entangled in compromising situations. The record of God's faithfulness to His every promise should encourage us as we hear God's call and find our role in His redemptive drama.

The promise to Abram and his descendants will be a constant refrain throughout the Old Testament drama. Israel was guilty of focusing on the promise of blessing rather than the call to be a blessing. The drama of blessing the nations to enable them to respond to their rightful King will become a consistent theme of the New Testament story and will come to its ultimate culmination at the return of the one true King and the healing of the nations (Rev. 21:22–26; 22:1–2).

For Memory and Meditation

"And I will make you a great nation, and I will bless you, and make your name great; and so you shall be a blessing." Genesis 12:2

Redeemed with Purpose

CHAPTER 5

FOCAL TEXT: EXODUS 3; 19

Few stories in the Bible are more beloved than that of the burning bush and the crossing of the Red Sea. They were immortalized by Cecil B. DeMille's epic movie, *The Ten Commandments*, about Moses' life. The exodus the key redemptive event in the Old Testament. The recounting of the history of Israel in the Old Testament frequently begins with this event. The early chapters of the book of Exodus recount the story of the redemption of a people, the birth of a nation, and a priestly commission.

The Context
Genesis 37–50; Exodus 1–2

The patriarchal period ends with the Israelites in Egypt. Jacob and his entire family came to Egypt as guests of Pharaoh during a time of great famine. The story of God's miraculous provision for Jacob's family is recorded in Genesis 37–50 and is well worth reading.

Joseph, the youngest of Jacob's twelve sons, is sold by his brothers to Midianite traders who took him to Egypt and sold him to Potiphar, the captain of the bodyguard of Pharaoh. Through a series of events that demonstrate Joseph's radical trust in God and God's sovereign care, Joseph is placed over the household of Pharaoh (Gen.

41). Joseph devises a plan to store up grain during a period of great abundance in preparation for seven years of famine. The famine provides the opportunity for Joseph to reunite with his family.. Because of the severity of the famine, Jacob reluctantly allows his sons to go to Egypt to buy food to keep his family from starving. On a subsequent visit Joseph reveals his identity to his brothers and secures an invitation from Pharaoh for Jacob's family to move to the land of Goshen in Egypt. God redeemed the evil actions of Joseph's brothers and place Joseph in a position to preserve His people (Gen. 50:19–21).

The book of Exodus begins with a listing of the names of the brothers who came to Egypt under Joseph's stewardship. While a small number of persons entered Egypt (seventy according to Exod. 1:5), they quickly multiplied and filled the land, a sign of God's blessing and the fulfillment of His promise to Abraham. Exodus 1 records a generational shift. We are simply told, "Now a new king arose over Egypt, who did not know Joseph" (1:8).

The new king, seeing the expansion of the Israelite people, devises a plan to keep them from becoming enemies and departing from the land. The "guests" now become "slaves" with the task of building storage cities at Pithom and Raamses (1:11). In spite of the affliction, the Israelites continue to multiply and spread out over the land. The king plans to stop the spread of the Israelites by killing all the male children. The midwives refuse to cooperate because they feared God so Pharaoh commands his people to cast every newborn son into the Nile. During this edict of death, Moses is born. His mother spares Moses' life by putting him in a basket among the reeds of the Nile. Pharaoh's own daughter finds the child and chooses to raise him as her own.

Once again we see the sovereign work of God, who is always at work fulfilling His promise and providing for His people. Moses is raised as a prince, having the unique advantage of an Egyptian education. In Acts, Luke records Stephen's message, which includes the story of Moses' education (Acts 7:22). God was preparing a leader who was capable of freeing his people and recording the story for all posterity. When Moses is forty (Acts 7:23), he is moved with intense emotion when he witnesses how the Egyptians are abusing his own people. He kills an Egyptian who is beating a Hebrew so Moses must flee for his life. The desire to save the Israelite was appropriate, but the action he took was wrong. Moses escapes to Midian where he marries Zipporah and becomes a shepherd.

The king of Egypt, the cruel taskmaster, dies; and the sons of Israel cry out to God in their bondage. "So God heard their groaning; and God remembered His covenant with Abraham, Isaac, and Jacob" (Exod. 2:24). Before the encounter at the burning bush, the deliverance of Israel is set in the context of the Abrahamic covenant— God promises, God remembers, God delivers.

The Divine Initiative
Exodus 3:1–10
Moses' shepherding duties are interrupted by a divine

messenger. The word "angel" means "messenger" and may signify an angelic messenger, or it may simply be a reverential way of speaking of God's presence. The blazing bush was a theophany or self-manifestation of God. Fire is often used as a symbol of God's presence in the Old Testament, signifying His holiness. God used the initial curiosity caused by a burning bush, which was not consumed, to arrest Moses' attention. The revelation, however, is not the burning bush but God's spoken word.

God's call is met by an immediate response, "Here I am" (v. 4). Moses doesn't doubt that God knows his whereabouts; he is responding to God's divine call. When Isaiah hears the voice of God in the temple, he responds, "Here am I. Send me!" (Isa. 6:8). Eli counsels young Samuel to respond to the voice of the Lord, "Speak, for Your servant is listening" (1 Sam. 3:10). The doctrine of God's calling is never impersonal, nor is it unrelated to man's obedience. God's call is personal, specific, and inviting.

God's first command to Moses is, "Do not come near here" (3:5). Moses is not yet prepared to enter God's presence or to understand His nature. He must first remove His sandals since He is standing on ground made by the presence of holy God. The removal of the sandals signifies the acceptance of the position of a servant, for a slave usually went barefoot (cf. Luke 15:22).

God first identifies Himself as the God of the patriarchs—Abraham, Isaac, and Jacob. Once again we see the connection between the exodus and the promise made to Abraham. Moses is not dealing with an unknown God but the God of Israel's history and heritage.

Moses will be privileged to bring a further revelation of the one true God known by their forefathers. He will no longer remain for this generation simply a God of the past; He will reveal Himself as the God who is active in their present and their future. Is your present-day faith and obedience sometimes affected because you have allowed God to remain a God of history?

This divine encounter was prompted by God's compassion for His people (v. 7) and His commitment to fulfill His covenant promise (v. 8). He has both seen the affliction of His people and has heard their cries (v. 9). For that reason He has "come down to deliver them" (v. 8) and to bring them to the land of promise that is here described as "flowing," or oozing, with milk and honey.

Moses' Mission
Exodus 3:10–12

God's plan to bring deliverance and provide a land is now revealed (v. 10). There is no contradiction between God's promise to deliver and His commissioning of Moses. We see once again the dynamic balance between God's sovereign activity on earth and the necessary and willing response of a human servant. God has chosen to accomplish His will and work on earth through His people who will join Him in His mission.

Moses' immediate response is one of unbelief as he cries, "Who am I, that I should go to Pharaoh, and that I should bring the sons of Israel out of Egypt?" (v. 11). Perhaps Moses was thinking about the consequences of returning to a place where he was guilty of criminal activity. Or possibly he was already thinking about his perceived lack of ability: "I am slow of speech and slow of tongue" (4:10). Self-distrust can be good if it leads to full reliance on the Lord; otherwise it can lead to spiritual paralysis and outright disobedience.

God's response is simple and profound: "Certainly I will be with you, and this shall be the sign to you that it is I who have sent you: when you have brought the people out of Egypt, you shall worship God at this mountain" (3:12). "I will be" is a play on the name YHWH, God's memorial name, explained in the following verses. Notice the assurance God gives to His "reluctant" missionary. He promises: (1) His presence, (2) a sign of affirmation which will only be visible when the task is completed, and (3) assurance of victory. The slaves will soon worship God as freed men on this mountain.

The Divine Name
Exodus 3:13–14

Moses expresses concern that the Israelites will not believe that he has been commissioned by the God of the patriarchs. Moses indicates they will want to know, "What is His name?" (3:13). This question does not suggest that the Israelites were unaware of the various titles of God as worshipped by their ancestors. Exodus 6:3 indicates they were certainly familiar with the name God Almighty (El Shaddai). The question concerning God's name on the part of the people would be the same as asking Moses what new revelation he has been given concerning the nature of God. Throughout the patriarchal days any new revelation of God would be summed up in a new title given by Him (16:13; 17:1; 22:14).

"God said to Moses, 'I AM WHO I AM'; and He said, 'Thus you shall say to the sons of Israel, "I AM has sent me to you"'" (3:14). The name YHWH is usually represented in most English versions as LORD in all capitals. The name comes from the verb "to be" in the Hebrew. It is tied to the idea of "life" or "being." The name communicates that God is absolutely self-existent. He is the One who in Himself possesses life and permanent existence.

Various commentators have suggested different translations of YHWH. The name is from the imperfect stem of the Hebrew verb "to be." The imperfect tense denotes an action that started in the past, continues in the present, but is not yet complete. I like the translation, "I AM who I have always been." God, who has commissioned Moses, is the same God who worked in the lives of Abraham, Isaac, and Jacob. He is the ever-present, incomparable God. However we translate the name, it affirms God's self-existence, His eternality, and His activity among His people. God's name demands a response of faith by Moses and the people of Israel.

The Priestly Nation
Exodus 19:1–9

We must fast-forward to Exodus 19:1–9 to see the rest of the story. God has fulfilled His promise of deliverance, and the sign He promised to Moses—the opportunity to worship Him at Sinai—has come to fruition. Moses ascends the mountain to hear from God. God first reminds Moses of His personal deliverance as He bore them on eagles' wings and brought them to Himself. The statement "brought you to Myself" (v. 4) is pregnant with meaning. Israel fully belongs to God. They were His by creation, and now they are His by redemption.

Israel is called to radical covenant obedience (v. 5) as God's unique possession among all the peoples. God has determined to commission and empower Israel to join Him in the task of restoring all nations to His kingly rule: "For all the earth is Mine" (v. 5b). God is constantly at work gathering the peoples of the earth under His kingly rule. Now Israel has been redeemed and called to join Him in this task. They are to be to Him "a kingdom of priests and a holy nation" (Exod. 19:5–6). They are to represent the King of kings as a people who obey His word, reflect His character, and advance His kingdom.

Israel failed to embrace this task and saw the blessing of God as something to be consumed rather than conveyed. With the coming of the Messiah, this task has now been given to His covenant community made up of all persons who enter into covenant with God through a personal relationship with His Son, the Messiah (1 Pet. 2:4–12). Are we fulfilling our task as a priestly nation?

For Memory and Meditation

"Now then, if you will indeed obey My voice and keep My covenant, then you shall be my own possession among all the peoples, for all the earth is Mine; and you shall be to Me a kingdom of priests and a holy nation." Exodus 19:5–6a

The God Who Speaks and Acts

CHAPTER 6

FOCAL TEXT: EXODUS 20

Most Bible students are familiar with the Ten Commandments, and many can recite them from memory. Yet there is more to the story than a simple list of "do's and don'ts." The giving of the law forms a critical link in the chain of God's redemptive and revelatory history. The law and the tabernacle speak of God's presence among and provision for His covenant people. The Ten Commandments reveal the character of holy God and are His gracious moral guidelines that will allow His people to worship Him and avoid sin. "Moses said to the people, 'Do not be afraid; for God has come in order to test you, and in order that the fear of Him may remain with you, so that you may not sin'" (Exod. 20:20).

The God Who Speaks
Exodus 20:1

The Ten Commandments or ten "words" are the beginning and the heart of Mosaic revelation. If you read chapters 21–23, you will discover that most of the ordinances contained in this section can be organized around the ten words. The commandments are found here and in Deuteronomy 5 where they are repeated for the new generation who will be privileged to enter the land promised to the patriarchs.

The entire section, beginning in chapter 19 with Moses' visit to Sinai, is set in the context of a covenant-making ceremony and a theophany or "appearing" of God. God was under no obligation to enter into a covenant relationship with His people, but He chose to do so. God's loving and gracious desire to relate to His people is a major theme of the entire Bible. We have already looked at the covenant God made with Noah and Abram. Those two covenants involved divine promises without the requisite human response. Noah and Abram were men of faith, but they did not earn God's covenant with their righteousness or faith. They were open to God's command and were willing to be directed by God.

The covenant in Exodus 19, following redemption from Egyptian slavery, is different in nature from those with Noah and Abram. The setting is not an affirmation of human faithfulness but a confession of God's redemptive activity. The oath or promise originates with God and demands the response of His people. They were to "obey My voice and keep My covenant" (19:5). Based on their response to God's requirement, they would be: "My own possession among all the peoples . . . a kingdom of priests and a holy nation" (19:5–6).

We are now entering the "theocratic period" of Israel's history. Theocratic comes from two Greek words when taken together mean the "the rule of God." At Mount Sinai, Israel became a theocracy, a people ruled by God. This period extends from 1445 to 1043 BC and is documented in the books of Exodus through Ruth. During this time God ruled directly over His people by way of His revealed law through prophetic spokesmen. This rule begins here with Moses, continues with Joshua, and is concluded with Samuel. There is no earthly king because God is their King, and they are His kingdom possession.

The Ten Commandments found in Exodus 20 are the conditions under which God accepts Israel as His people—a covenant type referred to as a "suzerainty" treaty. Verse 1 deliberately connects the phrase "all these words" to "God spoke." These words or commandments are a revelation from God. The emphasis is on source, purpose, and content. This section does not reflect a human attempt to appease and thus relate to God, but it demonstrates God's grace as He reveals His moral nature and provides moral imperatives that will enable man to worship God, live in dynamic relationship with his fellowman, and avoid sin.

The God Who Acts
Exodus 20:2

The phrase "brought you out" speaks of God's redemption action, which signaled the beginning of Israel's unique relationship to God. This simple phrase reminds us of the declaration in Exodus 19:4, "You yourselves have seen what I did to the Egyptians, and how I bore you on eagles' wings, and brought you to Myself." Pharaoh wasn't eager to release his workforce, nor was he shaken by Moses' demands to release the people of God. The Egyptians had a pantheon of gods—among them,

Pharaoh himself.

No, this was a cosmic showdown between a multitude of false gods and the one true God. God's purpose was bigger than the release of a single nation. God has Moses tell Pharaoh, "But, indeed, for this reason I have allowed you to remain, in order to show you My power and in order to proclaim My name through all the earth" (9:16). God is active in all of history gathering His people, scattered abroad by their attempt to create a name for themselves (Gen. 11:4). The tower of Babel signifies man's continuing attempt to achieve godlike status by human achievement. A beginning step in this global restoration is to bring a people to Himself to join Him in His redemptive activity.

Don't miss the final phrase of Exodus 19:4, "brought you to Myself." The God of Israel is no distant, impersonal God. He is a God of love and grace who redeems His people and provides for their every need. Even more, He remained with them each step of their journey, permitting them to experience Him through worship. He not only wanted them free from slavery; He wanted them with Him.

But God's people were not just to enjoy His presence; they were to be His earthly representatives, His "kingdom of priests" would join Him in the restoration of all the nations to their rightful relationship with their Creator and King. The phrase "for all the earth is Mine" looks to the day of restoration when His special people, His "own possession," would become a blessing to all nations.

God's unique claim on Israel was born out of His activity of bringing them out of slavery. Israel was His by creation, and now they are His by redemption. In Exodus 20:2, the word *LORD* in capital letters translates the name Yahweh, the name disclosed to Moses at the burning bush. The God of Israel is the living, dynamic, and active God. He is the only God who speaks and acts. All that follows in terms of commandments and ordinances is based on God's redemptive acts and Israel's unique privilege to represent the only true God among the nations. This verse makes clear that the law is set in the context of grace from its inception.

The Commandments Reveal the Nature of God and the Requirements for His People
Exodus 20:3

Israel would be known among the peoples of the earth because of their relationship with Yahweh. Their identity, authority, and nobility would be wrapped up in their unique position with God. Their role would be to extend the rule of the King throughout the earth. To accomplish this task, they must reveal God's name by embodying His character. In other words, to represent a holy God, Israel must be a holy people. Simply put, God redeemed Israel to be the showcase of His greatness on the earth and among the peoples of the earth. They were to be known by the glory of God that shown through them.

While the primary meaning of holy is to be "set apart" in terms of service, we can readily see why it must also mean "holy" in behavior and lifestyle. The God we serve is holy; and if we are to showcase Him to the world, we must reflect His holiness. This generation of Israelites would fail to respond to this calling to represent God among the peoples, and thus God would reaffirm this calling to a new generation. "For you are a holy people to the Lord your God, and the Lord has chosen you to be a people for His own possession out of all the peoples who are on the face of the earth" (Deut. 14:2). The thrust of the book of Leviticus is holiness for a people on mission with God. "You shall consecrate yourselves therefore and be holy, for I am the Lord your God. You shall keep My statutes and practice them; I am the Lord who sanctifies you" (Lev. 20:7–8).

As free moral agents who had entered into a covenant relationship with God, the people were to give themselves wholly to the task of holiness. As they submit themselves to God for His use, He would sanctify them. As they obey His commandments, God sets His people apart for mission. It was true then, and it is true now.

The first four commandments focus on Israel's undivided loyalty to the one true God. Israel lived in the midst of a polytheistic world, and these Commandments deal with the issues that face every person. The first command is straightforward: "You shall have no other gods before Me" (20:3). This does not affirm the existence of other gods as the Second Commandment makes clear. The prohibition against idolatry makes clear that any "gods" they might turn to would be those that were made with human hands. The term translated "before Me" literally means "to My face." The same term is used for taking a second wife while the first is alive. The relationship with God is so intimate and personal it can be spoken of in terms of marital love, and to seek other gods would be adulterous. Since they are to manifest God's name—His character—His name must not be profaned through their attitude and behavior. Their attitude toward labor and rest are to reflect the nature of their God.

The final six words focus on man's relationship to his family and his fellowman. It is obvious that one's love for God must be shown by the reality of one's love toward all persons created in God's image. Jeremiah would later state that caring for the afflicted and needy is what it means to know God (Jer. 22:16). Jesus speaks of the requirement of loving one another with the same passion that He loved His disciples as a "new commandment" (John 13:34; 15:12). When questioned by a lawyer about the Great Commandment in the law, Jesus summarized the entire list of the Commandments by making love of one's neighbor as essential to authentic faith as loving God with one's entire self.

A Modern-Day Priestly People
1 Peter 2:5, 9–12; Romans 12:1;
Hebrews 13:5–6

As a priestly people who represent holy God among the nations, Israel is called to a higher standard of living, which is clearly reflected in the Ten Commandments and the various statutes laid out in the book of Leviticus.

Peter applies the entire imagery of this section of Scripture to the church built on the cornerstone, which is Christ. "You also, as living stones, are being built up as a spiritual house for a holy priesthood, to offer up spiritual sacrifices acceptable to God through Jesus Christ" (1 Pet. 2:5). Later Peter calls us "a chosen race, a royal priesthood, a holy nation, a people for God's own possession, so that you may proclaim the excellencies of Him who has called you out of darkness into His marvelous light; for you once were not a people, but now you are the people of God" (vv. 9–10a). He then challenges his readers to live in such a manner among the Gentiles (nations) that the people will observe their behavior and glorify God (vv. 11–12).

Israel failed to embrace their task to join the King in the redemption of the nations. They *consumed* God's blessings rather than *conveying* them. The task of extending God's kingdom by representing Him among the nations has become ours. As a priestly people we are to bring living sacrifices to Him. Among these are our bodies (Rom. 12:1), our worship (Heb. 13:5), our service (Heb. 13:6), and our witness (Rom. 15:16). We must not view this high calling simply as a matter of privilege; it must become our passion.

For Memory and Meditation

"I am the Lord your God, who brought you out of the land of Egypt, out of the house of slavery. You shall have no other gods before Me." Exodus 20:2–3

Rebellion
and Restoration

FOCAL TEXT: JUDGES 1-2

The period of God's direct rule over Israel ends with the ministry of Joshua. The tenor of the book of Joshua is one of victory, freedom, and abundance as Israel occupies the land promised to the patriarchs. In contrast the book of Judges shows Israel in a downward spiral. They are in defeat, bondage, and decline. In Joshua they possess the land, but in Judges they are the oppressed people of the land. Those who had seen the hand of God in victory are now attempting to gain and sustain victory by human strength. As a result, much of the land that had been given to the twelve tribes of Israel is now in the hands of the Philistines and the Amalekites.

The books of Judges and Ruth record the period between theocratic rule (the direct rule of God through Moses and Joshua) and the beginning of the monarchy with Saul and David. The story of Ruth provides the one bright spot in an otherwise gloomy period. Hers is a story of loyalty and purity in a time of disobedience and immorality.[1]

The poignant book of Judges records a cyclical pat-

---

1 Norman L. Geisler, A Popular Survey of the Old Testament (Grand Rapids: Baker Books, 1977), 101. I am greatly indebted to this fine work in the organization of my material.

tern of sin and its accompanying oppression followed by God's gracious deliverance. Tragically God's goodness is spurned as Israel rebels time and again. Seven cycles of sin, bondage, supplication, and deliverance cover a period of nearly 380 years. In this book we will see three important themes: (1) Disobedience or partial obedience leads to oppression and bondage. (2) God is long-suffering in His love and desires to deliver and restore His people. Thus He responds to the prayers and repentance of His people. (3) A theocratic nation needs a righteous king. Thus the period of the Judges serves as a bridge to and an explanation for the establishment of a monarchy.

The judges do not primarily have a legal function as the title might imply. Typically, judges serve as a military deliverer—a statesman-redeemer. The various judges differ in skill and style, but each alike is given unique abilities that are recognized to be endowments from God, the one true Judge (11:27). The period of the judges demonstrates man's need for a righteous King. As we will discover in our study of the period of the earthly monarchy, this need will be perfectly fulfilled only in the coming of the Messiah, the "righteous One."

The Death of Joshua and Israel's Collective Memory
Judges 1:1–2; 2:6–10

Verse 1 introduces both the book of Judges and the period of the judges with the simple statement, "Now it came about after the death of Joshua." As you read verses 1–5, you will notice that they actually deal with events that occurred during the lifetime of Joshua, and thus they are intended to provide the background of the entire book and period of time in Israel's history. They tell the story of the initial success of inhabiting the promised land.

In response to the enquiry as to which tribes shall lead in the conquest of the Canaanites, the Lord responds; "Judah shall go up; behold, I have given the land into his hand" (v. 2). The term "Canaanites" is often used to designate all the inhabitants of the land at the time of Israel's conquest. Notice that the victory is assured by the Lord who declares that He has given the land into the hands of Judah. Many battles remain to be fought, but the final outcome has already been assured. Once again we see the unique conjunction of God's sovereignty and man's response and participation as God accomplishes His purposes through His people.

We return to the story of Joshua's death in chapter 2:6–10. Verse 6 indicates that the united campaigns under Joshua's leadership had broken the back of the Canaanite resistance. The importance of Joshua's leadership is clearly seen in the declaration: "The people served the Lord all the days of Joshua, and all the days of the elders who survived Joshua" (v. 7a). This generation of Israelites had seen "the great work of the Lord which He had done for Israel" (v. 7b).

Joshua died and was buried in the territory of his inheritance. At his death Joshua is celebrated as "the servant of the Lord" (v. 8). This same designation was applied to Moses and will be applied to David and many of the prophets. It suggests a call to a special mission. There is no higher call than to be the servant of the Lord; it was true then, and it is true now.

The beginning of the tragedy that led to rebellion and oppression is documented in verse 10. Joshua and the generation involved with the conquest died and "there arose another generation after them who did not know the Lord, nor yet the work which He had done for Israel." Israel could not simply rely on the faith of their fathers; a living faith must be personally embraced by each succeeding generation. Compromise with paganism was always an abiding temptation for Israel; and when Joshua's generation of faithful men died, the new generation did not embrace the living faith of their fathers or the memories of God's great deliverance.

Every generation must share the dynamic of their faith with their children to ensure that the memory of God's mighty work passes alive from generation to generation.

An Angelic Message and a Failure to Respond
Judges 2:1–5, 11–15

The Lord confronts Israel with the enormity of their sin, declaring that they have disobeyed God by making covenants with the people of the land and failing to tear down the pagan altars (v. 2). The phrase "the angel of the Lord" is regularly used to denote the manifestation of the Lord. Recall that the presence of the Lord throughout the wilderness period was associated with the tabernacle and the ark. The sanctuary has been moved from Gilgal, between the river Jordan and Jericho, to a more suitable location at Bochim; and thus it would be natural to say, "The angel of the Lord came up from Gilgal to Bochim" (v. 1) as a means of indicating God's presence with Israel.

God's presence, His deliverance from Egypt, and His faithfulness to His covenant (v. 1) makes Israel's rebellion stand out in stark relief. The emphasis throughout this section is on Israel's failure to abide by the terms of the covenant they had made with God. Remember the covenant was not unconditional but was contingent on Israel's obedience (Exod. 19:5). They had been reminded of the conditions of the covenant before they entered the land: "In that I command you today to love the Lord your God, to walk in His ways and to keep His commandments and His statutes and His judgments, that you may live and multiply, and that the Lord your God may bless you in the land where you are entering to possess it" (Deut. 30:16).

The tragedy of Israel's rebellion is summarized in a few short words: "But you have not obeyed Me" (v. 2). We can hear the shock in the question posed to Israel: "What is this you have done?" How could Israel turn their backs on the one true God who had delivered them from bondage and chosen them as His own people? Israel discovers that sin always has consequences. The people of the land will be a constant nuisance, and their gods will be a snare to Israel (v. 3).

Confronted with their sin, Israel lifted up their voices and cried out to God (v. 4). Their tears are so profuse they called the place Bochim, which means "weepers." Yet their actions make clear that while Israel wept, they did not repent. Superficial tears of "regret" are not the same as genuine repentance. Verses 11–15 demonstrate the lack of true repentance and the accompanying consequences. For several generations Israel's history can be summarized with four words that occur with cyclical regularity—*rebellion*, *servitude*, *supplication*, and *gracious deliverance*.

Verse 11 provides a succinct summary of their rebellion: "Then the sons of Israel did evil in the sight of the Lord and served the Baals." Baal, the son of El in the Canaanite pantheon, was believed to be the god of the storm and the rains and thus responsible for vegetation. Ashtaroth, the female consort of Baal (v. 13), was the goddess of war and fertility. As one might imagine, the worship of these fertility gods was often sexual in nature and thus led to other acts of lascivious rebellion.

God's righteous anger (vv. 14–15) had profound consequences as the Lord gave them over to their own design and desires. God gave them into the hands of their enemies, and they were defeated. No longer under the favorable hand of the Lord, they were "severely distressed" (v. 15). God used the surrounding nations to chastise His own people with the desire that they would return to Him.

It seems impossible to imagine that a people who had been chosen, delivered, and uniquely blessed would turn to gods that had no power. Yet do we not see the same tendency in our own lives? Do you ever find that you forget the gracious deliverance of the Lord? Does that knowledge lead to rebellion or repentance?

God's Gracious Redemption
Judges 2:16–19

In spite of Israel's rebellion, God responded according to His own nature. "Then the Lord raised up judges who delivered them from the hands of those who plundered them" (v. 16). These statesmen-deliverers were empowered by God to deliver His people from bondage (v. 18). We would hope that the long-suffering grace of God would be sufficient to cause Israel to return to God, but such was not the case. During and after the ministry of each judge, Israel failed to listen; and they returned to their false gods, playing the harlot with them (v. 19). Israel, called to be the bride of the Lord, had turned to the fertility gods of the Canaanites. This graphic imagery of adultery, as a violation of the covenant of a marriage relationship, demonstrates the intimacy God desires with His own people.

The rebellion of Israel increased in intensity when a judge died. Verse 19 indicates that Israel would turn back and act more corruptly each time they experienced deliverance. The nature of sin is cumulative and progressive. The voice of conscience can be dulled by successive acts of sin, and one can be led to believe that God's long-suffering mercy means that God is unaware or unconcerned about our sin. Man is continually tempted to use almighty God as little more than a lifesaver during times of emergency and then ignore Him when the crisis has passed. Have you seen evidence of this same pattern of behavior either nationally or individually?

The period of the judges is well summarized by the final verse. "In those days there was no king in Israel; everyone did what was right in his own eyes" (21:25).

An Enduring Promise
Judges 2:1

I may be getting a little ahead of the story, but I find it hard to leave this study without underlining a promise that brings hope even into this period of rebellion and captivity. The message delivered by the angel of the Lord contained these words: "I will never break My covenant with you" (2:1). When disobedience and rebellion led to punishment and captivity, God was still faithful to His covenant and still working for Israel's redemption.

Not only did God provide judges during this dark period, but He later sent prophets who would plead with Israel to return. God's faithfulness to His covenant led Him to work through a purified remnant, preparing the way for a new covenant, sealed by the death of His Son. With a clear voice we can celebrate the truth that gives hope—God will never break His covenant!

For Memory and Meditation

"Then the Lord raised up judges who delivered them from the hands of those who plundered them." Judges 2:16

The Building
of a Nation

FOCAL TEXT: 1 SAMUEL 7:15–8:9; 2 SAMUEL 7:12–16

The book of Judges ends with the somber note: "Everyone did what was right in his own eyes" (21:25). The author believed this behavior was directly related to the lack of a king to keep everyone in line. His assessment proved to be not entirely true, for the monarchy deteriorated and showed itself to be no remedy for man's sin and its evil impact on the land. Further, Samuel, the final judge and not the first king, led in the initial improvement in moral conditions. Samuel, a priest, was also the last of the judges. He bridges the gap between the turbulent period of the judges and the relative stability under the first kings.

The books of 1 and 2 Samuel were placed together as one book in the Hebrew Bible. First Samuel is basically about Saul, while 2 Samuel is about David. The people are located in the land of Palestine, and their religious life centers first around Jerusalem, captured by David (2 Sam. 5:7), and later around the temple built by Solomon (1 Kings 6). These books are important because they chronicle the story of the beginning of the monarchy and the divine origin of the Davidic dynasty.[1]

---

1 Norman L. Geisler, A Popular Survey of the Old Testament (Grand Rapids: Baker Book House, 1977), 108.

Samuel: A Bridge from the Judges to the Kings
1 Samuel 7:15–8:9

While the book of Samuel begins with the phrase, "Now there was a certain man" (1:1), the central character of the first few chapters is a woman. Hannah, the wife of Elkanah is childless. She is a devoted follow of the Lord and a woman of prayer. Being greatly distressed over her condition, she petitioned the Lord with a vow. If the Lord would provide a son, she would "give him to the Lord" (1:11) for a lifetime of service.

Woven into the tapestry of these first three chapters, which tell of Samuel's birth and dedicated service to the Lord, is the sad account of the fall of Eli's house. While serving as a priest to Israel at Shiloh, Eli failed to serve as a priest to his own sons. Eli knew about the sins of his sons and attempted to bring correction, but his sons would not listen to the voice of their father (2:22–25). The dissipation of Eli's sons is contrasted with the boy Samuel who "was growing in stature and in favor both with the Lord and with men" (2:26).

Samuel's divine call was recognized as his prophecies rang true and, "All Israel from Dan even to Beersheba knew that Samuel was confirmed as a prophet of the Lord" (3:20). During this period the Philistines defeated Israel and captured the ark of the covenant, the symbol of God's presence among His people (4:10). When Eli, who had been judging Israel for forty years, heard the news of the death of his sons and the capture of the ark, he fell backward from his seat and broke his neck (3:18).

Samuel seized the opportunity to call Israel to return to God with all their heart, put away their foreign gods, and serve God alone (7:3). Israel put away their idols and gathered at Mizpah to fast and repent. "And Samuel judged the sons of Israel at Mizpah" (7:6).

Verses 15–17 serve as a summary statement for the life of Samuel. After traveling to various cities to judge Israel, Samuel would return to his home in Ramah and worship God. Samuel intends to pass on the mantle of leadership to his sons and thus appoints them judges over Israel (8:1). "His sons, however, did not walk in his ways, but turned aside after dishonest gain and took bribes and perverted justice" (8:3).

For parents to fail to communicate their spiritual values to their children is tragic. Vital commitment in one generation often becomes mere form for the next and finally farce for succeeding generations. While we cannot decide for our children, we can teach and model those things that are most important to us. Samuel's children chose a different path from their father, and it altered history. The failure of Samuel's sons was one factor that led Israel to desire an earthly king.

A King like All the Nations
1 Samuel 8:4–9

A delegation of the elders visits Samuel at Ramah demanding a change in the existing form of government. They give two reasons for their request: Samuel's age and his sons' failure to walk in the ways of their father.

"Now appoint a king for us to judge us like all the nations" (8:5). In verse 20 we discover that the desire for a king emanated from their conviction that a king could protect them from oppressive enemies (cf. 1 Sam. 12:12). Samuel must have wondered if Israel had spiritual amnesia. Throughout Israel's history every human attempt to obtain victory had met with failure. Samuel was grieved by the request, seeing the desire for a king as spiritual rebellion since Israel was a nation ruled by God.

When Samuel seeks the face of the Lord, the Lord instructs him to listen to the voice of the people and give them what they want (8:6). God places this singular rebellious request in the context of Israel's continuous habit of forsaking the one true God to serving other gods (8:8). In this light Israel's desire and demand for a king is one event in a long line of rebellion and rejection of God's rule over a people He had redeemed and called to Himself (cf. Num. 14:11). The Lord instructs Samuel to give the people what they desire along with a solemn warning of the consequences of the decision to have an earthly king (8:9). Often the punishment for our sin is getting what we desire.

Samuel dutifully warns the people about the high cost associated with an earthly king: (vv.10-18) The decision to have a king would not simply add one person to the circle of political power; it would involve the establishment of an expensive bureaucratic institution that would consume personal and family resources (vv. 11–13). To sustain a growing bureaucracy, the king would require the "tithe" of their harvest and their flocks and make the people little more than his servants (vv. 15–17). The "tithe" was holy unto the Lord, but now it would be required by an earthly king. Unlike the heavenly King who delivered them and gave them status as a chosen people, the earthly king would bring oppression and humiliation.

In spite of the dire warning, the people of Israel declare, "No, but there shall be a king over us, that we also may be like all the nations" (8:19b–20a). God tells Samuel to give the people what they want. Thus was ushered in a troubling and turbulent future for Israel. In answer to Israel's demand for a king, the Lord gives them Saul.

Saul is first described by his impressive physical attributes; he is a handsome and imposing man who stands head and shoulders above all other men (9:1–2). He is skillful in battle and gracious in victory. Yet he is from the tribe of Benjamin, one of the most depraved tribes of the period of the judges. Further, he proves to be pastorally incompetent, spiritually disobedient, and often emotionally unbalanced. Saul, through his disobedience, establishes the truth that "to obey is better than sacrifice" (1 Sam. 15:22). The portrait of Saul foreshadows the sad outcome that awaits Israel under his leadership.[2]

We can take several lessons from Israel's rebellious desire for an earthly king: (1) It demonstrated a spiritual rebellion against the rightful rule of God. (2) It was based on the desire to conform to the pattern of other nations. (3) Therefore it denied their unique status as a people

---

2 *Description taken from Robert D. Bergen,* The New American Commentary: *1, 2 Samuel (Nashville: B&H, 1996), 118.*

chosen by God. (4) Their choice of a king was based on physical, not spiritual, criteria. Thus they chose a king from the wrong tribe. Israel had previously declared that "the scepter shall not depart from Judah, nor the ruler's staff from between his feet" (Gen. 49:10).

The Establishment of the Davidic Throne
2 Samuel 2:4, 7; 5:1-4

The book of 1 Samuel closes with the burial of the bones of Saul and Jonathan at Jabesh (31:13), and the book of 2 Samuel begins with David's learning of Israel's defeat and the deaths of Saul and Jonathan. With the death of the king and his son, there was a no functioning government in Israel. Abner, Saul's cousin and commander of Saul's army, and David, Saul's son-in-law and a leader of an army of his own, soon emerge as leaders.

David had faithfully served King Saul even after Samuel had anointed him as Saul's replacement (1 Sam. 16). David asks the Lord for guidance as to how and when he should establish his rule (2:1). The Lord instructs David to go up to Hebron. This was the tribal territory of David's ancestors and the location of the people most likely to support him as he ascended to the throne. Some of those who joined David in this place may have witnessed David's original anointing by Samuel. The Lord's previously revealed plan for David to shepherd His people had begun but only in limited fashion. Only those with blood ties to David were present at the anointing in Hebron (2:4).

Abner, the commander of Saul's army, installs Ish-bosheth the son of Saul over the remaining tribes of Israel. Conflict between the houses of Saul and David erupts, and civil war ensues. Throughout the two-year war, "David grew steadily stronger, but the house of Saul grew weaker continually" (3:1). All credible opposition to David's kingship ended with the deaths of Abner and Ish-Bosheth. All the tribes of Israel come to David at Hebron declaring that he is one of them and had been their leader even while Saul was king (5:1–2). They remember that the Lord had already anointed David as their shepherd-ruler (5:3). The words of the prophecy declare that the people of Israel are "My people" (5:2), indicating that they were chosen and redeemed by God alone. No earthly king could claim them. Second, David's role is to be a shepherd-ruler. He is appointed by God to defend, lead, and tend to the needs of God's flock.

All the elders make a covenant with David at Hebron, establishing him as king over all Israel and Judah. David was thirty when he became king, and he ruled for thirty-three years (5:4–5). Saul had been the people's choice while David was God's choice. David begins his united reign by capturing Jerusalem and leading the people to install the ark in the city of David. David's military conquests lead to great expansion. A rule that began with such promise is brought down by David's sin and shame as he covets another man's wife and then compounds his sin by having her husband put to death. The Bible does not gloss over the sin of the heroes of the Bible, a sure evidence of its truthfulness.

An Anointed King Who Will Reign Forever
2 Samuel 7:12–16

David's great desire was to build a permanent house for the ark, a place where God's name and fame would be clearly manifest (7:1). The Lord tells David that he will not be allowed to build a house for Him but that He plans to build a house (dynasty) for David (v. 11). "I will raise up your descendant after you, who will come forth from you, and I will establish his kingdom. He shall build a house for My name, and I will establish the throne of His kingdom forever" (vv. 12b–13).

Viewed in its immediate context, a portion of this promise was fulfilled by Solomon, who constructed the temple in Jerusalem between 966 and 959 BC (2 Kings 6). This promise of a King and an eternal kingdom runs through the remainder of God's Word. New Testament writers confirm that Solomon fulfilled a part of this prophetic promise (Acts 7:47), but they further affirm that the primary application of this verse was to Jesus, the ultimate "son of David" (Matt. 1:1). Only One who is eternal can establish a kingdom that will last forever. Jesus declares that He will build a temple (Matt. 26:61), sit upon an eternal throne (Matt. 19:28–29), and establish an imperishable kingdom (Luke 22:29–30).

For Memory and Meditation

"I will raise up your descendant after you, who will come forth from you, and I will establish his kingdom. He shall build a house for My name, and I will establish the throne of his kingdom forever." 2 Samuel 7:12b–13

The Kings and God's Kingdom

CHAPTER 9

FOCAL TEXT: 1–2 KINGS; 1–2 CHRONICLES

The books of Kings are so named because their chief subject is the kings of Israel and Judah. The books of 1 and 2 Kings provide a prophetic perspective on the royal leadership of Israel and Judah. The "political history" is a consequence of this effort. They provide a historical record of the main acts of the kings of Israel and Judah from the glory of Solomon's united kingdom to the shame of the divided kingdom, which led ultimately to humiliating Babylonian captivity. These books introduce us to the ministry of the prophets.

First Chronicles covers roughly the same period as 1 and 2 Samuel while 2 Chronicles covers the same period as do 1 and 2 Kings. The two books of Chronicles focus on the history of the temple and the religious history of Judah. Chronicles is written from a priestly point of view, emphasizing the role of the priests and the theocratic line of David in Judah. Any references to the northern tribes are tangential to the story line of these two books. There is also an absence of references to the prophets in contrast to the two books of Kings. In the Chronicles we see three compelling truths: God's faithfulness to His promises, the power of the Word of God, and the centrality of worship to the life and vitality of God's people.

Although the monarchy appears to thrive under the wise leadership of Solomon, who builds the temple and expands the kingdom, his success is short-lived; and the monarchy is divided between the northern ten tribes who make Samaria their capital and the southern kingdom centered in Jerusalem. While the general tenor of this period is one of rebellion and division, we again discover that God is faithful to His Davidic covenant.

The United Monarchy under Solomon
I Kings 1–11

Toward the end of David's life, Nathan the prophet discovers Adonijah has declared himself king (1:11) and is gathering support from the king's sons and the commanders of the army (1:25). David had promised Bathsheba her son Solomon would succeed him (1:13). The preemptive move by Adonijah to seize the throne is revealed to Bathsheba by Nathan. Bathsheba informs the king, who reaffirms his promise: "Surely as I vowed to you by the Lord the God of Israel, saying, 'Your son Solomon shall be king after me, and he shall sit on my throne in my place'; I will indeed do so this day" (1:30).

David moved quickly to frustrate Adonijah's plot by immediately installing Solomon as king. David summons Zadok the priest, Nathan the prophet, and Benaiah, the warrior and son of Jehoiada, and instructs them to put Solomon on David's mule and bring him to Gihon where they will anoint him as king over Israel (1:32–34). Mules were traditionally reserved for royal families (2 Sam. 13:29). Zadok took the horn of oil from the tent of meeting and anointed Solomon as king. The oil mentioned here was the sacred olive oil compounded by Moses (Exod. 30:23) and preserved in a ram's horn in the sanctuary tent. The anointing of Solomon led to a celebration that shook the earth (1:38–40).

David's charge to Solomon, found in 2:1–4, is given even greater solemnity by the fact that they were his dying words. The word translated "charged" has the impact of a last will and testament. He charges David, "Be strong, therefore, and show yourself a man" (v. 2). Strength of character was essential to one who would lead Israel. This strength was no ordinary strength; it comes from obedience to all that God commands. The use of a multiplicity of terms such as statues, commandments, ordinances, and testimonies indicates the comprehensiveness of this call to obedience.

The results of such radical and complete obedience will be twofold. First Solomon will succeed in all that he does (v. 3). The blessing of God accompanies the obedience of man. Second, obedience will ensure God's continual pleasure with the family of David, which means the promises, articulated in 2 Samuel 7:1–17, will be fulfilled including the eternal nature of David's kingdom. This promise was not only important to David; it is vital to every generation of believers who depend on David's messianic descendant for salvation and eternal life.

Solomon moves quickly to solidify his rule and expand the extent of his rule by creating an alliance with Pharaoh, king of Egypt. The Lord appeared to Solomon during the night in a dream and asked him what he desired from God (3:5). Solomon prefaces his request with the acknowledgment that his own rule is the result of God's faithfulness in fulfilling His covenant with David.

Solomon humbles himself before the Lord, acknowledging his own unworthiness. "Now, O Lord my God, You have made Your servant king in place of my father David, yet I am but a little child; I do not know to go out or come in" (3:7). He admits that he is staggered at the immensity of the task of leading God's people, whose greatness is measured by the fact that they were chosen by God. They are now so numerous they cannot be numbered or counted (v. 8).

Given the enormity of the task and the lack of experience of the petitioner, Solomon requests "an understanding heart to judge Your people to discern between good and evil" (v. 9). "Understanding heart" can be translated "a listening heart" or "an obedient heart." Only those who obey have truly heard (cf. Jas. 1:22). Solomon must obey God if he is to lead others to keep God's commands. Only by listening to God will Solomon have the capacity to listen to the people he is called to lead.

God is pleased that Solomon has made a request that will enable him to minister justly to others and has not asked for personal privileges such as long life and riches. Thus God promises to give him a wise and discerning heart unlike anyone who has ever lived. Further, He promises to give him riches and honor (v. 13). This final promise is based on the condition that he continues to walk in God's way and keep His statues and commandments. The conditional nature of Solomon's kinship is repeated each time God addresses Solomon directly (6:11–13; 9:3–9; 11:11–13). God's covenant with David is eternal, but Solomon can be replaced by another "son of David" if he fails to obey the Lord.

A crowning accomplishment of Solomon's reign is the building of the temple (chs. 6–8). The description of the temple makes clear that it was glorious in scope and adornment. Yet when Solomon stands to dedicate the temple, he first acknowledges the greatness and singularity of God who has kept the promise made to King David (8:22–27). Solomon is so overwhelmed by the majesty of God that he realizes the inadequacy of any human building to express or contain the glory of God. "But will God indeed dwell on the earth? Behold, heaven and the highest heaven cannot contain You, how much less this house which I have built!" (8:27). The temple exists not for God but for men's prayer and praise. If you read the remainder of chapter 8, you will discover multiple calls for repentance and prayer. The effect of such concerted and effectual prayer will be that "all the peoples of the earth may know Your name, to fear You, as do Your people Israel" (8:43).

A reign that began with so much promise ended in shame. Solomon, lured by his desires "loved many foreign women" (11:1) who were from nations God had instructed the sons of Israel to avoid because "they will surely turn your heart away after their gods" (11:2). This warning, unheeded by Solomon, led to his downfall. "For when Solomon was old, his wives turned his heart away after other gods; and his heart was not wholly devoted to the Lord his God, as the heart of David his father had been" (11:4). To appease his wives, Solomon built high places to accommodate the worship of these false gods.

Because of Solomon's disobedience, God indicates that He will tear the kingdom from him and give it to his servant (11:11). Only one thing keeps Solomon and his sons on the throne, and that is the promise made to David in 2 Samuel 7:1–17. Because of God's covenant with David, this tearing of the kingdom will not happen in Solomon's lifetime and will not be total. God promises to give a fragment to Solomon's son for the sake of David and for Jerusalem, which He has chosen (11:13). In spite of Solomon's sin and Israel's rebellion, God remains faithful to His covenant promise.

The Divided Kingdom
1 Kings 12–22

The fall of the united monarch was the result of immorality and idolatry that corrupted the kingdom from within. The resulting disunity was the practical outworking of spiritual corruption.

After Solomon's death Rehoboam, the son of Solomon, goes to Shechem where all Israel is prepared to make him king (12:1). Jeroboam has returned from Egypt and become a spokesman for the people. To understand the dynamics of the situation, we must look back to the latter half of chapter 11. Jeroboam, a valiant warrior, had been appointed by Solomon to oversee all the forced labor of the house of Joseph (ch. 28). While traveling from Jerusalem, he encounters the prophet Ahijah, who tells him that he will rule over ten tribes from the kingdom that would be torn from the hand of Solomon (11:26–39). Solomon apparently hears of the prophecy, and Jeroboam is forced to flee to Egypt (11:40).

Now that Solomon is dead and Rehoboam is ready to ascend the throne, Jeroboam returns from Egypt. As a spokesman for the people, he asks the king to lighten the load that has been placed on them by Solomon (12:4). Rehoboam wisely consults with the elders who had served his father. They advise him to serve the people and speak kindly to them with the promise that the people will then follow him (v. 7). He foolishly rejects their counsel and takes the advice of some young men who grew up with him. He informs the people that he plans to make conditions worse than they had been under his father (12:6–15).

Rehoboam's foolish response causes the people of the ten northern tribes to conclude that they have no portion left in David's inheritance. They make Jeroboam king over Israel (12:20) with only the tribe of Judah following the house of David (12:20). Jeroboam establishes centers of idolatrous worship in Dan and Bethel for fear the people will go to Jerusalem for worship and be tempted to return to Rehoboam. He makes two golden calves and says to the people, "It is too much for you to go up to Jerusalem; behold your gods, O Israel, that brought you up from the land of Egypt" (12:28).

Throughout 1 and 2 Kings two threads are continually intertwined—the morality of the kings and the ministry of the prophets. All the kings of the northern kingdom are wicked. Among the early kings of Judah, many are evil with only a few notable exceptions such as Asa and Jehoshaphat. Amid idolatry and corruption it is refreshing to read: "Asa did what was right in the sight of the Lord, like David his father" (15:11).

We encounter two important prophets in 1 Kings. Jehu is called to pronounce judgment on the house of Baasha, a northern king who did evil in God's sight (16:7). The most dominant prophet is Elijah who must confront Ahab, another northern king. Wicked King Ahab became notorious for his evil, exceeding all who had served before him (16:30). The final act of rebellion came when Ahab married Jezebel and they provoked the Lord by their aggressive idolatry (16:31). Much of Elijah's prophetic ministry, such as the prediction of the drought and the confrontation on Mount Carmel, was specifically related to God's judgment on Ahab.

The early kings did little to stop the moral decline of Israel. In truth all the kings of the north and all but two of the kings of Judah were evil rulers. The clear message of this first book of Kings is that the kingdom would prosper only if the king would respond to the message of God through His prophets.

For Memory and Meditation

"Keep the charge of the Lord your God, to walk in His ways, to keep His statues, His commandments, His ordinances, and His testimonies, according to what is written in the Law of Moses, that you may succeed in all that you do and wherever you turn." 1 Kings 2:3

Division, Deterioration, and Deportation

CHAPTER 10

FOCAL TEXT: 2 KINGS

Have you ever witnessed a sports team, organization, or a church with great potential lose their direction and impact because of division and internal deterioration? Tragic, isn't it? In this section we have a ringside seat to witness the tragic results of disobedience that leads to moral decadence and ultimately to the deportation of both Israel and Judah. God raised up prophets to call His people to repentance so they could avoid final doom, but the warnings went unheeded.

The northern kingdom, composed of ten tribes, was ruled by a succession of twenty kings from nine different dynasties; and all of them did what was evil in the Lord's sight. Judah has only twelve kings all from the dynasty of David according to God's promise. Six of those kings did what was pleasing in God's sight, and for that reason Judah avoids deportation to Babylon for more than a century after the northern kingdom falls.

The Continual Deterioration
2 Kings 1–17

An Example from the North (1:1–17)
The Moabites, perennial and powerful enemies of

Israel, were the descendants of Lot's grandson Moab (Gen. 19:30–38). They shared a border with Israel to the East of the Jordan and north of the Dead Sea. They were subdued under the leadership of the judge Ehud (Judg. 3:30). Once Ahab was defeated at Ramoth Gilead, the Moabites took advantage of Israel's weakness and came against Israel again. This occurred during the reign of Ahaziah (1:1–2).

Ahaziah, possibly because of the shocking news concerning Moab's rebellion, fell through the lattice in his upper chamber, which was in Samaria. He promptly sends messengers to inquire of Baal-zebub, the god of Ekron, to see if he will recover from his illness. The deterioration of the Israelites' faith is clearly seen when the king sends messengers to a pagan shrine to consult with a pagan deity rather than turning to the one true God. Baal-zebub is a localized version of Baal of Syria. The ending "zebub" means "a fly"; the name literally is "lord of the flies." The name may suggest that Baal-zebub was believed to be a god who warded off plagues brought on by flies. Can you imagine that persons who had seen God at work in great power would turn to pagan deities?

The messengers of the king are met by the great prophet Elijah who asks them why they have been dispatched to Ekron with the stinging question, "Is it because there is no God in Israel?" (1:3). He sends the messengers home with the news that the king will not recover from his illness. The messengers do not know the identity of the prophet, but from their description (1:8) the king knows that it is Elijah the Tishbite.

On three occasions the king sends messengers to instruct the prophet to come down to the king. Three times the prophet refuses, and each time fire rains down from heaven. Military might is no match for the power of God! At the instruction of the angel of the Lord, Elijah delivers the message of condemnation in person (1:15–16). The final epithet is simple and sad: "So Ahaziah died according to the word of the Lord which Elijah had spoken. And because he had no son, Jehoram became king in his place" (v. 17a). Ahaziah's weak and evil reign lasted only two years. He allowed Moab to rebel, he injured himself in a clumsy fall, he foolishly attempted to use military force against the spokesman of the Lord, and he sought help from a pagan god. Tragically a similar pattern is repeated by each of the northern kings.

A Bright Spot in the South (ch. 11–12)

Judah was ruled by only one queen. Athaliah was the daughter of Ahab and Jezebel. She was one of the most unscrupulous and brutal rulers in Judah's history. When her son Ahaziah was assassinated, she attempted to slaughter all her grandchildren so she could take the throne. Her plot was foiled by Jehosheba, the daughter of King Joram who hid Joash the son of Ahaziah in the house of the Lord for six years (11:1–3).

In the seventh year of Athaliah's reign, Jehoiada, the priest, convinces the temple officials and military personnel to crown Joash the rightful king of Judah (vv. 4–12). A celebration ensues that included loud clapping and shouts of "long live the king." The queen is seized, taken out by the lowly horse's gate, and put to death while Jehoiada leads the people in a covenant reaffirming their commitment to be the Lord's people (vv. 13–17). This renewal led to an immediate campaign to rid Israel of the blight of Baal worship (v. 18).

Joash began to rule when he was only seven years of age and ruled for forty years in Jerusalem (11:21–12:1). Joash's greatest and only recorded accomplishment was the repair of the temple, which had been grossly neglected. Solomon's grand temple was now about 140 years old. But age was not the only contributor to the dilapidated condition of the temple. The chronicler tells us that Athaliah and her wicked sons "had broken into the house of God and even used the holy things of the house of the Lord for the Baals" (2 Chron. 24:7).

Joash instructs the priests, "All the money of the sacred things which is brought into the house of the Lord, in current money, both the money of each man's assessment and all the money which any man's heart prompts him to bring into the house of the Lord, let the priests take it for themselves, each from his acquaintance; and they shall repair the damages of the house wherever any damage may be found" (12:4–5). The use of "assessments" (cf. Lev. 27:2) and "the money which any man's heart prompts him to bring" indicates two different categories of giving. Assessments would be equivalent to the tithe while the prompting of the heart would be a freewill offering above the tithe. Our giving should always begin with the tithe as a minimum standard but move beyond that as we are motivated by love. "God loves a cheerful giver" (2 Cor. 9:7).

Twenty-three years went by, and the repairs to the temple had not been made, so Joash takes matters into his own hands. He takes the responsibility for collecting the money from the priests and assigns it to the king's scribe. Joash has a chest with a hole in its lid placed in a prominent place by the altar, giving the project both visibility and priority. The money was guarded, counted, and given to the builders who were doing the work on the house of the Lord (vv. 9–12). Careful accountability seems to have been a contributing factor to the success of the offering. It is an interesting footnote that the king who grew up in the temple led the campaign to restore it. Did positive memories from early childhood prompt the repair?

This bright moment in Judah's history ends with a sad note. Syria under King Hazael attacks Jerusalem (12:17). To avoid the invasion, Joash sends all the sacred things and the gold of the treasuries of the house of the Lord to Hazael. Victory followed by defeat seems to be the continuing history of the southern kingdoms. In spite of Joash's strong leadership in the restoration of the temple, he failed to remove the high places, and the people still offered sacrifices there (12:3).

The Deportation of Israel (ch. 17)

Chapter 17 marks the beginning of the end. One lesson we can take from 1 and 2 Kings is that disobedience to God's law will bring sure judgment. The last king of the north was Hoshea. His reign is described in one short but poignant verse: "He did evil in the sight of the Lord, only not as the kings of Israel who were before him" (v. 2). While he was not as evil as the preceding kings, the cumulative effect of Israel's sin led to their ultimate defeat at the hands of Assyria.

The description of Israel's fall is briefer than the explanation for why it occurred. Two short verses describe the total collapse of the north (vv. 5–6). We are told that the king of Assyria besieged it three years, captured Samaria, and carried them away, settling them in Halah and Habor.

Verse 7 begins the explanation for the deportation; it is not a list of military failures but of spiritual ones. Israel's rebellion dates back to the time of the exodus. Israel should have served God faithfully because they remembered that He had redeemed them and treated them with favor, making them His own possession. Thus the first sin on the historian's list is spiritual ingratitude streaming from Israel's failure to remember God's grace.

The list continues by itemizing one sin after another from verses 7–17. Among the sins listed are: feared other gods, walked in the customs of other nations (v. 8), attempted to hide their sins (v. 9), built high places of worship (v. 9), and set up idolatrous pillars and images and burned incense to them (vv. 10–12). Nonetheless, the Lord who is long-suffering sends warnings through His prophets and seers who call God's people to turn from their evil ways and obey God (v. 13). "However, they did not listen, but stiffened their neck like their fathers, who did not believe in the Lord their God" (v. 14). This led to radical disobedience (vv. 15–17).

Verse 18 is brief but final: "So the Lord was very angry with Israel and removed them from His sight; none was left except the tribe of Judah" (v. 18). The northern kingdom was taken into captivity in 722 BC. Verse 19 gives us a preview of what is soon to come. Judah was following the same path that led to the downfall of the northern kingdom. This fate is briefly stayed by the powerful ministry of prophets like Isaiah and Jeremiah.

The Assyrians leave some of the Israelites behind and fill the city with men from foreign lands. This sets the stage for the development, through intermarriage, of a people called the Samaritans. Thus ends the story of the northern tribes, one characterized by idolatry and immorality.

The Deportation of Judah
2 Kings 18–25

The final half of 2 Kings treats only the history of Judah since Israel is in captivity. While there are a few bright spots, this section shows the continual decline of the southern kingdom. In this final period Judah is ruled by two good kings—Hezekiah and Josiah—along with six evil kings.

Hezekiah begins his twenty-nine-year reign with much promise. The historian notes: "He did right in the sight of the Lord, according to all that his father David had done" (2 Kings 18:3). Among his accomplishments was the removal of the high places and objects of fruitless worship, which included the bronze serpent Moses had made (v. 4). We should all desire that verses 5–6 could be written about us. He trusted in the Lord, clung to Him, and did not depart from following Him.

Hezekiah enjoyed military success, waging an aggressive war against the Philistines (18:7–8) and throwing off the yoke of tribute the Assyrians had afflicted on Judah. When threatened by the Assyrian king, Hezekiah tore his clothes, donned sackcloth, and humbled himself before the Lord (19:1). He is encouraged by Isaiah the prophet (19:6–7), pours out his heart before God (19:14–19), and receives an answer of God's sufficiency (19:20–37).

Josiah clearly possessed the faith of his great-grand-father Hezekiah. At the tender age of sixteen, he inaugurates a great revival that leads to many reforms. In the course of his temple duties, Hilkiah, a priest, found the law of Moses, which had been lost in the house of God (22:8–10). When confronted with the Word of God, Josiah repents (22:11–13). He then gathers the people at the temple, reads the law, and leads the people to enter into a covenant of obedience (23:3). This act was followed with sweeping reform including doing away with idolatrous priests (23:5), destroying the Asherah (23:6), and tearing down high places (23:7–8).

Josiah is the last of the godly kings of Judah. He is mentioned in both Jeremiah and Zephaniah. His untimely death in 609 BC was a mere four years before Israelites, perhaps including noblemen such as Daniel (although he may have been deported later), began to be deported into captivity. Josiah's third son, Jehoahaz, ruled only three months after the death of his father. He was removed from the throne by Pharaoh Neco who installed another son of Josiah, Jehoiakim, as king (23:34–37). Jehoiakim reigned for a little over a decade, during which time Judah was invaded by the Babylonians under the leadership of Nebuchadnezzar. During this time, around 605 BC, Israelites from Judah first began to be deported to Babylon.

Jehoiachin, son of Jehoiakim, succeeded his father on the throne and reigned only three months. He also did evil in the sight of the Lord (24:9). Nebuchadnezzar besieged Jerusalem, and Jehoiachin surrendered the city. He, along with other select noblemen of Judah such as Ezekiel, was deported to Babylon. The Babylonians installed Zedekiah, the remaining son of Josiah, as king in name only (24:17–20). In futility he attempted to rebel against Nebuchadnezzar. As a result, Jerusalem was burned and plundered. "Thus precisely as it was predicted, Zedekiah saw the invading king (Jer. 34:3). His eyes were put out [after watching his sons murdered] (2 Ki. 25:7), and then he was taken to Babylon, a land he would not see (Ezek. 12:13). This fateful date [was] 586 B.C."[1]

For Memory and Meditation

"Now this came about because the sons of Israel had sinned against the Lord their God, who had brought them up from the land of Egypt from under the hand of Pharaoh, king of Egypt, and they had feared other gods." 2 Kings 17:7

---

1 Norman L. Geisler, A Popular Survey of the Old Testament (Grand Rapids: Baker Book House, 1977), 145.

Exile to Babylon: Being God's People in an Alien Land

CHAPTER 11

FOCAL TEXT: LAMENTATIONS; EZEKIEL; DANIEL

God's people in captivity! If no god exists apart from Yahweh the Covenant God of Israel, how can we understand God's people in bondage? Can one still serve God faithfully in an alien land? These and many other questions must have plagued the people of God as they were ingloriously carted off to Babylon.

Three Old Testament books were written during the time of captivity that helped God's people deal with the past and look to the future with hope. Lamentations, whose Hebrew title is taken from the word "how" and whose title in the Greek means "tears of Jeremiah" is a lamentation over the destruction of Jerusalem and the temple. It was written to express sorrow for the destruction of Jerusalem and to remind Israel of God's constant love. It stresses both God's faithfulness to His promise to punish sin and yet maintain His steadfast love for His people. Daniel and Ezekiel look forward to future restoration. Daniel, as a prophet, looks forward to the political restoration of Israel as a nation whereas Ezekiel takes a priestly view and anticipates the spiritual restoration of the temple.

Grieving for the Past While Looking to the Future
Lamentations
The Sorrows of Zion and its Cause
(1:1–5, 8, 18)

The theme of the book is established in these opening verses, which graphically describe the calamity that has overtaken the southern kingdom and its capital city Jerusalem. In normal times Jerusalem was a busy commercial center, but now the city is empty. "How lonely sits the city that was full of people! She has become like a widow who was once great among the nations! She who was a princess among the provinces has become a forced laborer!" (1:1).

To show the utter devastation of the city, the author employs the image of widowhood. This image is employed frequently in the Old Testament to picture the depths of human loneliness and despair. The writer will use several other images to depict the total devastation of Jerusalem—a weeping daughter (ch. 2), an afflicted man (ch. 3), tarnished gold (ch. 4), and a fatherless child (ch. 5).

The fall is graphically portrayed by the image of a princess who has now become a slave (v. 1b). Little wonder she weeps bitterly at night (v. 2). Again in 3:48–49 the sense of overwhelming grief and pain is pictured in the weeping of God's people. "My eyes run down with streams of water because of the destruction of the daughter of my people. My eyes pour down unceasingly, without stopping."

Judah finds no comfort from her lovers, and her friends deal treacherously with her (v. 2b). Jeremiah used the phrase "her lovers" to refer to nations such as Egypt, Tyre, and Sidon, with whom Judah sought to ally against Babylonia. These friends failed her miserably. Rather than turning to God in repentance, Judah attempted to find a military solution to a spiritual problem.

The roads that were once filled with pilgrims coming to Jerusalem for the appointed feasts are empty (v. 4a). "Gates" describes the area just inside the city wall where justice was meted out by the elders and merchants sold their wares to busy shoppers. The city has ceased to function.

While the description is graphic and moving, we must now consider how and why this happened. "For the Lord has caused her grief because of the multitude of her transgressions" (v. 5b). This is restated in verses 8 and 18. "Jerusalem sinned greatly, therefore she has become an unclean thing. . . . The Lord is righteous; for I have rebelled against His commands." A righteous God must punish sin, and that punishment has taken the form of captivity.

A Cry of Hope (3:21–25)

Jeremiah, the author of Lamentations, remembers God's mercy and His faithfulness to His covenant promises, and it gives him hope for the future. "The Lord's lovingkindnesses indeed never cease, for his compassions never fail. They are new every morning; great is your faithfulness. 'The Lord is my portion,' says my soul, 'Therefore I have hope in Him'" (vv. 22–24).

An important Hebrew word (hesed) is used here to speak of God's loyalty to His covenant promises. The author speaks of the limitless nature of divine mercy. This unchanging constancy of God provides a firm foundation for hope in the midst of captivity. Every believer has a living hope because he/she is assured that God's promises are as sure as His judgments.

A Prayer for Restoration (5:19–22)

"You, O Lord, rule forever; Your throne is from generation to generation. Why do You forget us forever? Why do You forsake us so long? Restore us to You, O Lord, that we may be restored; renew our days as of old" (5:19–21).

Anticipation of Political Restoration and More Daniel

Daniel sought to encourage the Jews to withstand the temptation to worship the pagan king and his false gods. His prophecies comforted and assured the exiled people that their nation would be restored and an eternal kingdom established by the rightful King. Daniel condemns the existing (beastly) powers of this world and promises that God has a plan to establish His kingdom, affirming that God is in control of all affairs of history.

God's People in an Alien Land (1:3–8, 17–20)

Daniel and several young men, including some of the royal family and nobles, were selected to serve in the king's court (v. 3). The criteria for selection (v. 4) enabled the king to select the best of the best. The youth were taught "the literature and language of the Chaldeans" (v. 4).

The study of Babylonian literature would lead these Jewish youth into a completely alien worldview. We find, however, no objection to the study of a polytheistic literature that included magic, sorcery, and astrology, which was banned by the law (cf. Deut. 18:10–12). These young men from Jerusalem had to be secure in their own faith not to be swayed by these pagan myths. No doubt, as children they had been instructed from the books of Moses. In order to bear an effective witness to God in an alien culture, these young men had to have a solid foundation of faith and had to understand the cultural presuppositions of those among whom they now lived.

The understanding of the Chaldean culture, however, did not mean accommodation or compromise of their own core convictions. The king appointed for them a daily ration from the king's table, which would have included foods not deemed to be clean (kosher) according to Levitical food laws. Further, portions of the wine and food were often offered to the Babylonian god before being sent to the king. These godly young men had to decide what was nonnegotiable in an environment unsympathetic to their religious convictions. Daniel's refusal to eat the food was based on deep religious convictions and his desire to remain true to God. Daniel politely asks that he be served a substitute diet (v. 8).

The Lord affirmed this bold stand by giving Daniel favor in the eyes of the commander of the officials who agreed to the plan (v. 11). They were tested for ten days, and each youth was found to be in better condition than those eating the king's choice food (v. 15). Because of God's favor these youths excelled in knowledge and intelligence (v. 17) so that they were found to be ten times better than all the magicians and conjurers in the realm (v. 20).

The courage to live counterculturally is seen throughout the book. When ordered to fall down and worship a golden image, the Jewish youth again stand firm even at the threat of death (ch. 3). When confronted by an edict that forbade prayer to anyone other than the king, Daniel entered his house, opened his windows, and prayed "as he had been doing previously" (6:10). These events must have encouraged fellow Jews to remain steadfast in their commitment to God in a hostile environment. We can learn much from Daniel in this regard.

The Coming Dissolution of the Kingdoms of This World and the Triumph of God's Kingdom (2:44–45; 7:13–14)

Through a series of visions, God revealed to Daniel how the kingdoms of this world would each be destroyed and God would establish His eternal kingdom.

Daniel alone is able to interpret Nebuchadnezzar's dream of a great metallic statue, which represents man's attempt at self-rule (ch. 2). Daniel tells him the vision shows the fall of earthly kingdoms such as Babylon, Medo-Persia, Greece, and Rome. Daniel declares: "In the days of those kings the God of heaven will set up a kingdom which will never be destroyed, and that kingdom will not be left for another people; it will crush and put an end to all these kingdoms, but it will itself endure forever" (2:44). He affirms that this dream is both true and the interpretation is trustworthy.

In chapter 7 Daniel has a dream with virtually the same content, but in this vision the earthly kingdoms are represented as beasts. The head of gold is the lion Babylon; the arms of silver are a ravenous bear (Medo-Persia); the thighs of brass are a vicious leopard (Greece); and the legs of iron are a monster (Rome). A horn (power) arises out of Rome (the antichrist) who rules until the coming of the Ancient of Days. The Ancient of Days sits on a throne ablaze with flames. A river of fire is flowing from His throne while myriads of people are standing before Him (7:9–10). As Daniel continues to look at his vision, "One like a Son of Man was coming, and He came up to the Ancient of Days and was presented before Him. And to Him was given dominion, glory and a kingdom, that all the peoples, nations and men of every language might serve Him. His dominion is an everlasting dominion which will not pass away; and His kingdom is one which will not be destroyed" (vv. 13–14). Daniel assures the disposed people of God that "the saints of the Highest One will receive" this kingdom and possess it forever (7:18).

The Coming of the Messiah (7:9)

One of the most amazing predictions in the Bible is found in Daniel. While meditating on the seventy years of captivity, predicted by Jeremiah (ch. 25), the angel Gabriel told Daniel that seventy sevens of years would pass before the Messianic Age would come. The first sixty-nine sevens (483 years) would run from the command of Artaxerxes to rebuild Jerusalem (445 BC) to the cutting off of the Messiah (crucifixion). Using lunar years (twelve thirty-day months = 360 days) we come up with 476 solar years, which takes us to AD 31, the time of the crucifixion of Christ. Even skeptical critics would admit this prophecy was given 165 years before Christ.

Anticipation of a Spiritual Restoration Ezekiel

Whereas Daniel was concerned about political kingdoms and the kingdom of God, Ezekiel focuses on the restoration of the temple and the religious system. Ezekiel continually counteracts false hopes for an early return to the promised land but assures God's people of a full and final restoration. The name Ezekiel means "strengthened of God." His focus throughout is on the glory of God, which assures judgment on sin and the vindication of His righteousness (11:12). Ezekiel repeats the phrase "for my name's sake" stressing God's faithfulness to His promises.

The judgment on evil is God's preparation for blessing. God's blessing will include the bestowal of new life (chs. 33–39) and the establishment of a new order (chs. 40–48). God's plan for ultimate restoration would begin with the physical act of allowing His people to return to the promised land. But God had in mind so much more.

God would raise up for Himself a people who would possess His Word in their hearts and not just on their lips. Yes, revival always begins with a righteous remnant. By cleansing His people (36:25), God would vindicate His name, which had been profaned among the nations (v. 23). God's plan is not simply to bring cleansing; He will give His people a new heart and put a new spirit within them (v. 26). He will put His Spirit within them, enabling them to obey His statutes (v. 27).

The results of God's radical open-heart surgery will enable His people to live permanently in His presence (v. 28), enjoy plenty (vv. 29–30), and join God in expanding His kingdom to all nations. This section ends with the promise, "Then they will know that I am the Lord" (v. 38). God's plan to gather the nations to Himself through the blessing of Israel will be renewed and expanded.

For Memory and Meditation

"One like a Son of Man was coming, and He came up to the Ancient of Days and was presented before Him. And to Him was given dominion, glory and a kingdom, that all the peoples, nations and men of every langue might serve Him." Daniel 7:13b–14a

Return and Restoration

CHAPTER 12

FOCAL TEXT: EZRA; NEHEMIAH; ESTHER

In spite of Israel's and Judah's great rebellion, God remains faithful to His covenant promises. These three postexilic books, with the story of the return and revival of God's people after seventy years of captivity (cf. Jer. 25:11; 29:10), demonstrate once more that all of history is His story.

Ezra and Nehemiah were one book in the original Hebrew. Ezra pays primary attention to the rebuilding of the temple and the restoration of the religious life of God's people. Nehemiah focuses on the rebuilding of the city. Ezra is divided into two sections. Chapters 1–6 tell of the return under Zerubbabel and the rebuilding of the temple, while chapters 7–10 document the return under Ezra and the rebuilding of the people. Esther falls between these two sections and deals with God's provision for the Jews who did not return after the exile.

A Promise Fulfilled
Ezra 1:1–5

Notice that biblical events are placed both in the context of world events and the divine will of God. The return from bondage occurred in the first year of the reign of Cyrus, king of Persia. Cyrus entered Babylon in

539, and this decree was given in 538 BC. Some critical scholars point out that from the fall of Jerusalem (587) to the first return (538) would not have fulfilled the prophecy of seventy years. If, however, we calculate based on the completion of the temple (516), we would have our seventy years.

We have corroborating evidence concerning the benevolent rule of Cyrus from sources other than Ezra and Nehemiah. The famous Cyrus Cylinder, a small clay cylinder found by archaeologists, has writings about Cyrus, including some of his own memoirs. This cylinder indicates that Cyrus had been welcomed in Babylon as a friend and that he sought to do good for the people under his reign. He rebuilt their dilapidated housing and sought to reestablish religions devastated by Babylon.

The cylinder contains an interesting and informative quote: "I returned to [these] sacred cities on the other side of the Tigris, the sanctuaries of which have been ruins for a long time, the images which [used] to live therein and established for them permanent sanctuaries. I [also] gathered all their [former] inhabitants and returned [to them] their habitations."[1] While Cyrus does not mention Jerusalem by name, he does indicate that he returned religious images stolen by the Babylonians. He rebuilt temples for those images and resettled displaced peoples.

Cyrus, according to his own testimony, did this to curry

---

1 Quoted from Mark D. Roberts, The Communicator's Commentary, Ezra, Nehemiah, Esther (Dallas: Word, 1993), 43. He uses the translation of J. B. Pritchard, ed., The Ancient Near East: An Anthology of Texts and Pictures.

divine favor. Isaiah provides a unique perspective on the matter. Isaiah writes that the Lord revealed to him Cyrus was His anointed leader to subdue nations (45:1). In verse 13 the prophecy becomes more specific: "I have aroused him in righteousness and I will make all his ways smooth; He will build My city and will let My exiles go free, without any payment or reward."

Cyrus's declaration in Ezra 1:2 agrees with Isaiah's understanding. No telling of history is neutral or objective; it is always told from one's worldview. Ezra and Isaiah give us a theological understanding of world events from the viewpoint that the sovereign God of Israel controls history. Cyrus declares that whoever desires to return to Jerusalem should go with God's favor (v. 3) and that "every survivor" (v. 4), whether they return or remain, should support the rebuilding of the temple with a freewill offering.

Verses 5–6 indicate that this is precisely what happened: those whom God had stirred their spirit left for the rebuilding effort while "all" encouraged them with a freewill offering. The specificity of this historical event is impressive as the gifts and the participants are listed in great detail in chapter 2. Chapters 3–6 tell the story of the rebuilding and the opposition by adversaries of the work. The work ceased for a short period until the prophets Haggai and Zechariah encouraged them to complete the work (5:1). The temple is completed and dedicated and the Passover is observed (6:13–22).

A Spiritual Restoration
Ezra 7:1, 6–7; 10:1–4

Several generations have passed between chapters 6 and 7, and religious zeal has waned. God raises up Ezra the priest to bring revival to the nation. He labored so that the people would once again know and obey the law. The author begins with Ezra's lineage to show that he was from the Aaronic high priestly line (7:5).

Verse 6 indicates Ezra's obedience to God's command, his knowledge of the law, and the blessing on his life. The term "skilled" indicates that Ezra was well versed in the law of Moses. God always prepares people for the unique task He has prepared for them (cf. Eph. 2:10). Ezra knew the law, and he knew how to apply it. While we are never told what Ezra requested from King Artaxerxes, we are told that he received it "because the hand of the Lord his God was upon him" (7:6; cf. vv. 9, 28). God not only prepares people to accomplish His work; He also empowers them to complete it.

More than 1,750 men returned with Ezra; many "leading men from Israel" (7:28). These men are listed in chapter 8. Ezra discovers that the people have intermingled with the people of the lands causing him to tear his garment and kneel to pray (9:3–5). The prayer of intercession recorded in chapter 9 is one of the great prayers of the Bible. Like Isaiah, Ezra identifies with the sins of the people: "Since the days of our fathers to this day we have been in great guilt" (9:7). He acknowledges God's righteousness and confesses that they have no right to stand before a holy God (9:15).

This prayer of confession and repentance is followed by a great revival. A large assembly of men, women, and children join him as they weep bitterly before the Lord (10:1). The people make a covenant with God, put away their foreign wives, and promise to obey God's Word.

God's Protection of His People
Esther

This book fits chronologically between Ezra 6 and 7. It was addressed to the Jews who did not return to rebuild the temple. It demonstrates the providential care of God for all of His people and provides the history behind the celebration of the feast of Purim (ch. 7).

The Persian king Ahasuerus (Xerxes) and his queen Vashti both give lavish banquets in which the wine must have flowed freely. When the heart of the king was merry with wine, he sent his eunuchs to summon Queen Vashti in order to display her beauty to the people (1:11). She refused, and the king, fearing that the women throughout the kingdom would rebel, deposed Vashti and began the search for a new queen.

The king's attendants suggest a beauty contest of young virgins from which a new queen could be chosen. Mordecia, a gatekeeper for the king, seizes the opportunity to recommend his cousin Esther (2:5–8). Esther quickly finds favor with the king and is placed above all other women. This position of honor allows Esther to keep Mordecia informed about events inside the palace. Haman, the captain of the guard, convinces the king that the Jews refuse to keep the laws of the king and should be destroyed.

When Mordecia hears of the plot, he immediately begins to fast and pray (4:1–3). Mordecia devises a dangerous plan that requires Esther to appear uninvited before the king. When Esther tells Mordecia of the potential danger of such a strategy, he replies; "Do not imagine that you in the king's palace can escape any more than all the Jews. For if you remain silent at this time, relief and deliverance will arise for the Jews from another place and you and your father's house will perish. And who knows whether you have not attained royalty for such a time as this?" (4:13–14). Mordecia is certain that God will deliver His people. The only remaining question is whether Esther will be the human vessel God uses. She is convinced that God has placed her in the royal palace for this moment in time. She calls on the Jews to fast and pray and indicates that she will go before the king even if he kills her (4:15–16).

Esther plans a banquet for the king and invites the wicked Haman. Haman's pride and anger become intertwined. He boasts about the favor he has found with the king but is angered because Mordecia does not fear him (5:9–14). Haman builds a gallows to have Mordecia put to death. In a surprising turn of events, Haman is hanged on his own gallows. On December 13, the day the Jews were to be destroyed, Haman and his sons were hanged. The king sent an edict prohibiting the killing of the Jews. Mordecia sent letters to all Jews requiring them to celebrate on the following two days (9:20–21). This was called the feast of Purim from the word Pur meaning "lots" since Haman had cast lots to determine which day to destroy the Jews.

The Reconstruction of the City
Nehemiah

Nehemiah was a contemporary of Ezra (Neh. 8:2, 9), a layman with a prestigious position. He was the cup-bearer to King Artaxerxes. Nehemiah's experience in the king's court uniquely prepared him for the physical and political reconstruction of Jerusalem. Nehemiah is another great man of prayer. When he is first confronted with the news that the people in Jerusalem are in great distress and that the walls and gates are in disrepair, he "sat down and wept and mourned for days" (1:4). He first acknowledges the greatness of God (1:5), confesses his and Israel's sin (1:6–7), affirms God's covenant promise (1:8–10), and determines to take action (1:11).

Nehemiah, like Esther, puts his life at risk by going before the king with a sad countenance. He informs the king of the conditions in Jerusalem and receives both his permission to return to help rebuild the wall and also his assistance (2:5–8). The king promises to provide the timber for the gates "because the good hand of my God was on me" (2:8). God provides for His people from many unique sources.

After inspecting the walls (2:11–16), Nehemiah solic-ited others to join him in the work by recounting how God had blessed him before the king (2:17–18). The people respond, "'Let us arise and build.' So they put their hands to the good work" (v. 18). Opposition is immediate and intense as men like Sanballat and Tobiah ridicule those who have chosen to work (2:19; 4:1–3). In each instance Nehemiah stays true to his calling and points the people to the activity of God (2:20). The internal opposition is equally challenging as some begin to complain about the cost of the project and the financial sacrifice it will require (ch. 5). Nehemiah once again prays and takes decisive action. He relieves the burden of the people and refuses to take his salary as governor (5:14).

In spite of opposition, the wall is completed and a census is taken which included the number of the people and a listing of the gifts they gave to help complete the wall (ch. 7). After finding a genealogical record, Nehemiah restores the people to the land that had been their family inheritance. Israel has once again occupied the promised land.

The physical work complete, the people gather as Ezra reads the law of Moses (8:1–3). Ezra and others explain the clear meaning of the word (8:7–8) so the people began to weep and mourn (8:9). Ezra tells them this is a time for celebration not mourning, "For the joy of the Lord is your strength" (8:10). The feast of booths is restored (8:13–18), the people confess their sins (ch. 9), and a great revival sweeps the nation. A result of true revival is always the renewal of one's vows to the Lord. The people make a written commitment to separate themselves from the evil of the land and obey God's laws (10:28–29). This includes a commitment to bring their firstfruits and tithes to the Lord.

Jerusalem is rededicated with appropriate festivity that reflects the people's joy and thanksgiving (ch. 12). The reading of God's Word accompanied by confession and repentance led to revival and covenant renewal. The revival led to sweeping social reforms, the cleansing of the temple, and a renewal of worship (ch. 13). God's people are once again in the Holy Land, awaiting the final fulfillment of Messianic prophecy.

For Memory and Meditation

"Thus says Cyrus king of Persia, 'The Lord, the God of heaven, has given me all the kingdoms of the earth and He has appointed me to build Him a house in Jerusalem, which is in Judah.'" Ezra 1:2

Epilogue
A Look Back—a Look Ahead

Throughout our study of the Old Testament, we have had a front-row seat to witness the sovereign care of God whose righteous love compelled Him to remain faithful to His covenant promises in the face of Israel's constant rebellion. We have seen God's desire to work in history through a people who embody His character, obey His Word, and join Him in His mission of the redemption of all the nations.

God created everything for His own purposes to reflect His glory. Man, the zenith of creation, was affirmed to be "in His image," meaning that he/she was a relational, rational, and responsible being. Man was designed to relate to other human beings, but more importantly he was capable of relating to his Creator. Man, who was given unlimited personal access to God in the garden, sought to be a god rather than serve the one true God. The fall had staggering consequences that continue to impact the whole of creation. In spite of man's rebellion and fall, God was continually at work protecting man from his own rebellion and seeking to bring him back into dynamic relationship with God, creation, and himself.

The staggering consequences of sin are seen in the utter dissipation that leads to judgment through the flood.

Holy God cannot tolerate sin and thus must bring judg-ment even though it grieves His heart. Even in the midst of judgment, we witness God providing for the redemp-tion of man. We see His desire to enter into personal covenant relationship with mankind.

The continual rebellion of man is seen in the building of the tower of Babel, which demonstrates man's desire to be his own god rather than to serve the one true God. To thwart man's futile efforts, God brought confusion into human communication and scattered the people over the face of the earth. God is tenacious and tender when it comes to the redemption of man, and thus He selects a man (Abraham) and a people (Israel) to join Him in the process of restoring all nations and peoples to their rightful King.

The period of the patriarchs, chronicled in Genesis, comes to an inglorious end as Israel treats their calling as privilege and not responsibility, resulting in slavery at the hands of the Egyptians. Once again God acts to redeem His people as He commissions Moses to lead Israel from bondage. Israel now belongs to God both by creation and by redemption. They are saved with the unique purpose of joining God in His redemptive activity. As a covenant people, a priestly nation, they are called to radical obedience.

God speaks directly to Israel through Moses, estab-lishing gracious moral guidelines that will allow His people to worship Him and avoid sin. The giving of the Ten Commandments signals the beginning of the "theocratic period" of the history of Israel. During this period God ruled over His people by means of His revealed law and through His earthly spokesmen, Moses, Joshua, and Samuel. Israel needs no earthly king because God is their King and they are His kingdom possession. Under the leadership of Joshua, Israel enters the land of promise.

Israel's sin and rebellion continues, and the people who once possessed the land have now become an oppressed people of the land. The period of the Judges demonstrates a cyclical period of sin and bondage followed by supplication and deliverance. This period demonstrates man's need for a righteous king. Thus begins the period of the monarchy, which will demonstrate that the need for a righteous king will only be fulfilled in the coming of the Messiah, the true "Righteous One."

Samuel is a unique figure who bridges the gap between the turbulent period of the judges and the relative stability under the first kings. Saul, the first king, was chosen because of Israel's desire to be like other nations, and thus the criteria used for his selection were primarily physical rather than spiritual. The rebellion of Saul leads to the choice of David and the establishment of the Davidic line from which the Messiah will come.

The last king to serve the united monarchy was Solomon. Solomon's success is short-lived, and the monarchy is divided between the ten tribes of the north who make Samaria their capital and the southern kingdom centered in Jerusalem. The general tenor of the period is one of rebellion and division, with a succession of corrupt kings. Nonetheless, God remains faithful to His covenant with David and preserves the Davidic kingdom in the south.

The period of the kings moves from division to deterioration and ends with deportation. The northern kingdom, ruled by a succession of twenty kings from nine different dynasties, was first taken into captivity by the Assyrians in 722 BC. The southern kingdom manages to survive until 586 BC because a few good kings such as Hezekiah and Josiah brought spiritual reform.

Three books—Lamentations, Ezekiel, and Daniel—were written during the time of captivity to help God's people deal with the past and look to the future with hope. In spite of Israel and Judah's great rebellion, God remains faithful to His covenant promises.

The books of Ezra, Nehemiah, and Esther chronicle God's sovereign care for His people. Some people return under Zerubbabel and participate in the rebuilding of the temple. Another group returns under Ezra and participates in a spiritual rebuilding project. The book of Esther chronicles God's activity in providing for His people who remain in captivity. Nehemiah, a layman, leads the rebuilding of the wall. God's people are once again in the Holy Land, awaiting the fulfillment of Messianic prophecy.

A Coming King and His Kingdom
Three postexilic prophets are raised up to call for a spiritual and moral reconstruction of the returned remnant. Haggai and Zechariah, who focused on the rebuilding of the temple, spoke primarily of the spiritual

and religious needs of Israel. Malachi spoke of the need for the accompanying moral and social reform. Zechariah's desire was to encourage the return remnant by showing that God was at work restoring Israel to their spiritual inheritance in preparation for the coming of the Messiah.

But words of hope had come even before and during the time of the exile from prophets like Isaiah, Jeremiah, and Ezekiel who spoke of a King and a kingdom that would never end. Isaiah is the most frequently quoted of the Old Testament prophets by the authors of the New Testament. He speaks of Messiah as Immanuel who is born of a virgin (7:14). He will be called "Wonderful Counselor, Mighty God, Eternal Father, Prince of Peace" (9:6), and there will be no end to His rule (9:7). He will come from the "stem of Jesse" (11:1), will be a Suffering Servant who will bear the sins of His People (53:1) and thus finally and fully deliver the captives (ch. 61).

To the weary-eyed inhabitants of burned-out Jerusalem, Jeremiah shouted welcome news. The streets and cities that have been in desolation will be filled with a sound of joy and gladness as the voice of the bridegroom and the bride shout out, "Give thanks to the Lord of hosts, for the Lord is good, for His lovingkindness is everlasting" (33:11). The days are coming when the righteous Branch of David will execute justice and righteousness on the earth (33:15), and the promise of a King to sit on the throne of the house of Israel forever will be fulfilled (33:17).

Yes, David's royal line may have had the earthly appearance of having been chopped off at the stump, but look—there was yet life in the stump. A shoot would spring forth, one whose kingdom would never end. We are now prepared for coming of Messiah—"The record of the genealogy of Jesus the Messiah, the son of David, the son of Abraham" (Matt. 1:1). We are prepared for a startling announcement accompanied by a call to spiritual renewal—"Repent, for the kingdom of heaven is at hand" (Matt. 3:2).